The
GRANDEUR
of
GOLGOTHA

The GRANDEUR *of* GOLGOTHA

Volume One of the TRIUMPH TRILOGY

Neil M. Fraser

GOSPEL FOLIO PRESS
P. O. Box 2041, Grand Rapids MI 49501-2041
Available in the UK from
JOHN RITCHIE LTD., Kilmarnock, Scotland

THE GRANDEUR OF GOLGOTHA
by Neil M. Fraser
Copyright © 2000
Gospel Folio Press
All rights reserved

Previously published by Pickering and Inglis Ltd., London, 1959

Published by Gospel Folio Press
P. O. Box 2041
Grand Rapids, MI 49501-2041
http://www.gospelfolio.com

ISBN 1-882701-65-8

Cover design by J. B. Nicholson, Jr.

All Scripture quotations from the King James Version unless
otherwise noted.

Printed in the United States of America

Publisher's Foreword

Where would we be without the cross of Christ? It is almost too horrific to imagine. The cross is man's only hope. It sets us free from the powers of darkness and opens heaven to us. It is the deathblow to the devil, the secret of victory over the flesh, and the gravesite of that great world system that is opposed to God (Gal. 6:14).

The cross tells us how matchless is divine mercy and how terrible sin must be. It is the supreme portrait of God's love for us, and at the same time exposes the vileness of that human hatred against Christ which was *"without a cause."* At Calvary, heaven and hell collided in a cosmic struggle, and heaven won the field.

Singlehandedly—*"by Himself"*—the Lord Jesus there *"purged our sins"* (Heb. 1:3), *"taste[d] death for every man"* (Heb. 2:9), and *"destroy[ed] him that had the power of death"* (Heb. 2:14). In His mighty cross work, our Champion laid the basis for redemption (Eph. 1:7), justification (Rom. 5:9), reconciliation (Col. 1:20), sanctification (Heb. 13:12), and our ultimate glorification.

In this wonderful little book, the author, in warm and eloquent ways, brings to our hearts a vast array of treasures that come to us from Golgotha. He shows us how poor we would be if the Lord Jesus for our sakes had not become poor. We consider the seven great words from the Saviour's lips; we marvel at the six miracles that unfold there. As well, the cross is seen in its work of putting to death the self life, the flesh, and the world; in the symbols of baptism and the Lord's Supper; in the proclamation of the gospel; and in its comforting and strengthening ministry in the believer's life.

Mr. Fraser went home to be with the Lord January 6, 1974. He has done a great service by bringing us again to the foot of the cross. If we sense that our love for Christ is not as it should be, if it is not as it was at the first, we can rediscover first love where we first loved Him—at Calvary.

J. B. NICHOLSON, JR.
Grand Rapids, Michigan

Author's Introduction

Each of us must dig and discover for himself that "wondrous cross" of which Isaac Watts wrote:

> When I survey the wondrous cross,
> On which the Prince of Glory died,
> My richest gain I count but loss,
> And pour contempt on all my pride.

Once we start digging, seeking for the cross as silver, and searching for it as for hidden treasure, we find that our mine is infinitely richer and deeper than we ever imagined, our mound yielding vessels of purest gold.

We only regret that our tools are so crude and our hands so clumsy that we fail to secure it all. We are straightened only in ourselves.

We can only pray that our unskillful hands may not have marred or defaced the treasure in any way, and that it has been unearthed for others who, perhaps not having time to search, have hearts to appreciate.

Neil M. Fraser
Eugene, Oregon
1959

Contents

ONE

The Divine Manifesto of the Cross

*From that time forth began Jesus to show unto His
disciples, how that He must go unto Jerusalem,
and suffer many things of the elders and chief priests and
scribes, and be killed, and be raised again the third day.*
MATTHEW 16:21

The two divisions of Matthew are indicated in the first
verse of the book: *"The book of the generation of Jesus
Christ, the Son of David, the Son of Abraham."* While the
words have reference to the genealogy contained in the
first chapter, they also draw attention to the offer of the
Kingdom to Israel by the Son of David, and then to the
"offering" of the Son of Abraham on the altar at Calvary.
One would have thought that the chronological order would
have been followed and our Lord declared to be the Son of
Abraham, the Son of David, but the divisions of Matthew
show the presentation of the King (chs. 1–4), the principles
of the King (chs. 5–7), and powers of the King (chs. 8–12),
followed by the parables of the King (ch. 13), after it has

been clearly indicated at the end of chapter 12 that the King will be rejected by His subjects. The climax is reached in chapter 16 when *"He left them, and departed"* (Mt. 16:4). Thereafter the Son of Abraham, of whom Isaac is the type, makes known His approaching death.

While the powers of the King go on after this, and the crowd cries, *"Hosanna to the Son of David,"* (Mt. 21:9) His other parables show the setting aside of Israel, and the inheritance given to others.

The prophecies of the Kingdom follow in chapters 24–25, when it is seen that the King is going away. But He will return again in glory, to the reward of those who are His by spiritual ties, and in vengeance on those who would not have this Man to reign over them.

His death is still the passion of the King (chs. 26–27): *"This is Jesus, the King of the Jews,"* (Mt. 27:37) but the scribe instructed in the kingdom of heaven can see that His death is that of a burnt-offering offered upon one of the mountains that God had told Abraham of (Gen. 22:2).

Out of his treasure the scribe brings forth things new and old—the fact that the newer truth of the presentation of the Son of David must give place to the older offering of the Son of Abraham (see Mt. 13:52). It is at the beginning of the second division that we have the first mention of the Church and the cross.

THE APPROACH TO THE CROSS

When Jesus came into the coasts of Caesarea Philippi, He asked His disciples saying, Whom do men say that I the Son of Man am? (Mt. 16:13).

It is in the coasts of Caesarea Philippi that we have these divine announcements. The very name and location proclaim the subservience of the land to the Gentiles, with Caesar and a Herod sharing the honors. Far removed from Judea, center of Israel, and amid the ruins of idolatry, in one of the most northern points of His mission, our Lord proclaims the building of His Church, and the deep death sleep of the Cross by which this Bride of Christ should be formed. Out of the nations He would select a people for His Name, and those that sat in darkness would bask in the sunshine and warmth of a love told out in the offering of the Son of Abraham.

"But whom say ye that I am?" (Mt. 16:15). These loyal friends of Jesus would not tell Him the worst that men said about Him, but the best—which only showed that the crowd did not know Him at all. Some said He was John the Baptist, for their Master displayed the same courage and bold denunciation of the forerunner. Others said Elijah, adding to the sternness of the Baptist the remembrance of mighty miracles. Some said Jeremiah, thinking of their Lord's sorrows and tears, while some again were more vague and opined He was one of the prophets. They had this in common, that He was One who was of old. They believed in resurrection.

But Jesus pressed for a testimony from His own. He was done with the nation as such for a time. His own were now those whom He would love to the end. Peter, speaking out for himself and doubtless for them all (Judas excepted), said, *"Thou art the Christ, the Son of the living God."*

Upon this foundation the Church is built, and wherever you have such a confession you have the members of that Church. Every living stone that is built into it has made the good confession, as 1 Timothy 6:12 assures us. Whosoever makes the same confession as Peter becomes a sanctuary for God. *"Whosoever shall confess that Jesus is the Son of God, God dwelleth in him, and he in God"* (1 Jn. 4:15).

"From that time forth" Jesus began to declare His approaching death. As soon as the Church was announced, that upon which it is built must be equally proclaimed. When we have the divine declaration that it was not good that Adam should be alone—that a help be found suitable for him—then we have the divine operation, the deep sleep of Adam. From a bone God made (built) a woman. The divine presentation follows, when the Lord God brought her to the man.

So it is here. The Church, the Bride of Christ, can only have being in the death of the cross, from the deep wounds of her Lord. She was to be bone of His bone, flesh of His flesh. It was not fitting that this Man should be alone in eternity. The presentation would come in that day when He would present to Himself a glorious Church not having spot or wrinkle or any such thing. All the movements of Genesis 2 are seen in Ephesians 5.

The Apprehension of the Cross

"Be it far from Thee, Lord: this shall not be unto Thee."

Our Lord's apprehension of the cross is clear in His utterances from the beginning. The shadow of the cross was always before Him. His knowledge of the prophetic Word and the sacrifices offered daily on the altar were acute and eloquent reminders of His approaching death.

One is impressed, however, with the fact that these utterances were at first more often addressed, not to His own disciples, but to His adversaries. It is His death at the hands of men. But it is from this time, on the confession of His Messiahship by the disciples, that He began to show them the deeper meaning of that death. From this point on there would be an increasing emphasis, an increasing vision of it, until the night in which He was betrayed. Then He would give them the bread and the wine, the symbols of His body and of His blood shed for the remission of sins. The impending death of the Son of David was one thing; the willing offering of the Son of Abraham was another, to be declared on the confession of the faith of Christ's own.

Peter, however, did not apprehend the cross at first. He who had but a short time before spoken by inspiration of God, now spoke by inspiration of Satan.

Be it far from Thee, Lord: this shall not be unto Thee. But He turned and said unto Peter, Get thee behind Me, Satan (Mt. 16:22–23).

The Spirit of God has put the two utterances of Peter on the same page of Scripture that we might learn how poorly the Church would be built were it dependent on Peter for its foundation. Not on the *petros* of Peter, but on the *petra* of his confession, the Rock, Christ Jesus was the Church built. Peter here was but a stumbling block in the path of Christ, a snare (*skandalon*) of Satan to turn Him from it.

"Tell me what Jesus said to St. Peter as recorded in St. Matthew, chapter 16," asked a Romanist of one who challenged the claim of the priest. He was astonished at the reply. "Get thee behind Me, Satan, thou art a stumbling block unto Me, for thou mindest not the things of God, but the things of men."

But Peter learned his lesson and the sufferings of Christ became his constant theme and confidence. It is interesting to see the different emphasis he gives to the cross in each chapter of his first epistle.

In 1 Peter 1, these sufferings are a necessity for the Scriptures, for they testified of them beforehand and of the glory that should follow. Peter discovered that there could be no other understanding of these prophetic portions.

In 1 Peter 2, these sufferings are a necessity for servants, for they are called to follow the steps of Christ, who when He was reviled, reviled not again; when He suffered, He threatened not. Our Lord, therefore, not only suffered to keep us ultimately from suffering, but to show us in the meantime how to suffer.

In 1 Peter 3, the sufferings are a necessity for sinners to bring them to God, changing them from enemies to friends, from unjust to justified ones.

In 1 Peter 4, the sufferings of our Lord are a necessity for all sufferers, particularly those suffering for Christ's sake, that they might not think that something strange was happening to them. They are partakers of His afflictions, the reproaches that fell on Him now falling on them.

In 1 Peter 5, these sufferings are a necessity for shepherds, who tend the flock of Christ. Peter bases his exhortation on being a fellow elder, a witness of the sufferings of Christ, and a partaker of the coming glory. They would best tend the sheep by following the Chief Shepherd who would reward all such effort with a crown of glory.

Thus the beloved apostle apprehends the cross and sees the necessity for the sufferings everywhere: in fulfilling the prophetic scriptures; in dealing with the issue of our sins; in enabling us to rejoice in our afflictions; in their pastoral character—displaying the sufferings of a shepherd for his sheep—all this and more Peter apprehended in the Saviour's cross.

THE APPLICATION OF THE CROSS

If any man will come after Me, let him deny himself, and take up his cross, and follow Me. For whosoever will save his life shall lose it: and whosoever will lose his life for My sake shall find it (Mt. 16:24-25).

With the announcement of His cross is the announcement of our own. The cross needs to be applied; it needs to be carried.

And as they led Him away, they laid hold upon one Simon, a Cyrenian, coming out of the country, and on him they laid the cross, that he might bear it after Jesus (Lk. 23:26).

"...Him they compelled to bear His cross" (Mt. 27:32). Blessed compulsion!

Charles Simeon was a college professor who endured much persecution and ridicule. It was fashionable in English universities then, as it is now, to treat Bible lovers with supreme contempt. On one occasion, sorely pressed by his adversaries, he sought the solitude of the woods and cried to God to give him a portion from the Book they so heartily despised. Opening his Greek Testament, his eyes fell on the words concerning Simon the Cyrenian. They came with startling application because of his own name. Then and there he called on God to lay the cross upon him afresh and henceforth he bound "affliction as a wreath about his neck."

Yet, in the last analysis, the bearing of the cross is something voluntary—some affliction, some labor, some suffering we could escape from, but bear for Christ's dear sake. It is not really the afflictions that overtake us, but those we take over, like the Master's decease (*exodus*), spoken of in the holy mountain, an accomplishment at Jerusalem, at the very center of the opposition (see Lk. 9).

We can save our lives, save ourselves that trouble, that investment of time and money for His cause, and learn later that we have lost our lives. Or we can lose our lives in the eyes of men, only to find that we have invested them in the best of all interests. It may be our blessed Lord does not compel the cross, but if He does, we shall find the same exultation as did Charles Simeon long ago.

God forbid that I should glory, save in the cross of our Lord Jesus Christ, by whom the world is crucified unto me, and I unto the world (Gal. 6:14).

TWO

The Significance of the Cross

He saved others; Himself He cannot save.
MATTHEW 27:42

There are several occasions in the Gospel records when the enemies of our Lord uttered truths, the deep significance of which was lost upon them. *"Perceive ye,"* they said, *"how ye prevail nothing? Behold, the world is gone after Him"* (Jn. 12:19). Their world was very small, very circumscribed. It could scarcely have gone beyond the limits of their own little country. They scarcely knew how the world, the whole length and breadth of it, the whole sanctified art and learning of it, for two thousand years, would go after Him. The best in music, the best in literature, the best in art, would find its inspiration and direction from the Man of Nazareth, the Lord of Glory. We rejoice today to be in the company of those who are still going after Him.

Again, *"Never man spake like this Man"* (Jn. 7:46).

These words were uttered by officers sent to arrest Jesus, but they were arrested themselves and forgot their mission in the charm and challenge of His words. And ever since that Prophet spake, books that cannot be numbered have been written to elucidate the meaning and gather the strength from the sayings of Jesus.

Caiaphas, we feel sure, did not recognize the full meaning of his own words which, in the eyes of the inspired Apostle John, became a prophecy of Christ's death, not only for Israel, but for other nations (see Jn. 11:49-52). Caiaphas' words end with verse 50 and the expediency that he saw in the death of Jesus for them (note *"you"* instead of *"us"* in RV) was, we judge, a political one and not spiritual. But John saw a significance and an opportunity to declare the scope and unifying power of that death.

"This Man receiveth sinners and eateth with them" (Lk. 15:2). The words were uttered in scorn, but they have become the very glory of the evangel of Christ committed to men. Wherever men have opened the doors of their hearts and homes He has come in to sup with them and they with Him.

But here is the greatest example of unwitting homage to our Lord in the supreme hour of His trial. God thus made the wrath of men to praise Him.

> *Likewise also the chief priests mocking, with the scribes and elders said, "He saved others; Himself He cannot save. If He be the king of Israel, let Him now come down from the cross and we will believe Him. He trusted in God; let Him deliver Him now, if He will have Him: for He said, 'I am the Son of God'"* (Mt. 27:41-43).

It is our sober conviction that the enemies of Jesus our Lord said the words tauntingly of themselves, temptingly of the devil, truthfully for God, triumphantly for the Church, and the writer would add, thankfully for me.

TAUNTINGLY OF THEMSELVES

They did not know they were fulfilling the prophetic word:

> *...a reproach of men, and despised of the people. All they that see Me laugh Me to scorn: they shoot out the lip, they shake the head, saying, "He trusted on the Lord that He would deliver Him: let Him deliver Him, seeing He delighted in Him"* (Ps. 22:6-8).

The words would have frozen upon many lips had they known. They were hurrying One away to death who had been an annoyance to them, who was spoiling their lucrative trade in the temple and their prestige with the people—One who exposed their hypocrisy and challenged their cherished traditions. They were anxious to wipe their hands of His blood and to go and celebrate the Passover with unleavened bread, indicating the blamelessness of their lives. So they mocked and jeered and taunted the Sufferer on the middle cross.

TEMPTINGLY OF SATAN

We believe if ever all the hosts of hell were marshalled together, it was that day at the place called Calvary. Satan was personally heading them, for it was he who entered into Judas and who doubtless hounded him to death after he had betrayed his Master. Behind the voices of the chief priests and scribes and elders, behind the mockery of the soldiers, the thieves, and all that passed by, was the voice of Satan. Four times after the same manner the enemies of Nehemiah sent him a message to come down from his building of the wall. His reply, in the light of the cross, deserves mention here.

I am doing a great work, so that I cannot come down. Why should the work cease, while I leave it, and come down to you? (Neh. 6:3).

The voices of the passersby, the chief priests and scribes, the thieves and the soldiers, were the subtle temptations of Satan shouted through the lungs of men. "Come down from the cross. You cannot! You cannot!" How Satan shouted it through the lips of those custodians of religion! And if Jesus had come down He would have triumphed in the eyes of the short-sighted onlookers. But the whole scheme of redemption would have failed. And prophets and priests and kings would have wept at the collapse of the fabric they had built up in preparation for the cross, and at the doors of heaven closed against the sons of men. Satan had spoken through the voice of Peter to turn our Lord from the cross; now the serpent's voice is heard again tempting Him to come down.

TRUTHFULLY FOR GOD

"He saved others." The Father's heart had delighted in that. Heaven had rejoiced over sinners repenting under the preaching of His holy Son. He had saved Nicodemus who came to Him in the night of his need (Jn. 3), who stood for Him in the rising twilight of testimony for Christ (Jn. 7:50), and who came out in the daylight of true consecration with his hands filled with fragrance for the body of Jesus (Jn. 19:39). Even in death our Lord's garments would smell of myrrh and aloes (Ps. 45:8).

He saved the woman at the well, who had met six men, but found nothing to satisfy her heart. She met a seventh, God's perfect Man, the Saviour of the world, the Christ, and she thirsted no more (Jn. 4).

He saved the woman, a five hundred pence debtor, when she got behind the divine creditor and wept. She went away with forgiveness, salvation, and peace, and without saying a word (Lk. 7). Aye, He saved others—saved them physically from blindness, deafness, dumbness, disease, and death; saved them morally from despair and grief; saved them spiritually from demons and defeat and damnation.

"Himself He cannot save." None knew that better than God. He came to do a work, and like Boaz, *"would not be in rest until He have finished the thing that day"* (Ruth 3:18). Foxes might rest in their holes and birds of the air in their nests, but the Son of Man had nowhere to lay His head. But that day, after He said, *"It is finished,"* He would lay (rest) His head upon His own breast and die. If He was to finish the work which demanded the shedding of blood for the remission of sins, He could not save Himself. And let us say reverently, God could not save Him either.

> Himself He could not save,
> He on the Cross must die,
> Or mercy cannot come
> To ruined sinners nigh.
> Yes, Christ the Son of God must bleed
> That sinners might from sin be freed. —*A. Midlane*

He cannot save Himself the stroke if His people are to be shielded. He cannot save Himself the distance if they are to be near to God forever. He cannot save Himself the darkness if they are to dwell in the light. He cannot save Himself the utter forsakenness of God, if they are to enjoy the welcome of the Father's house. Oh, what a glorious witness, however unintentional, was raised for God that day in Jerusalem.

TRIUMPHANTLY FOR THE CHURCH

How believers have exulted in the truth! Christ saved the inquiring eunuch, the persecuting Saul, the pious

Cornelius, the hardened jailer, the thieving Onesimus, the eloquent Apollos, the profligate Augustine, the sagacious Alfred the Great, the deceived Luther, the scholarly Faraday, the enslaved John Newton, and a multitude no man can number. Blessed truth! He saved others.

"Himself He cannot save." In the words often attributed to Major Andre, found on his person after his death during the American Revolution:

> On Him Almighty vengeance fell
> That must have sunk a world to hell;
> He bore it for a sinful race,
> And thus became their hiding place.

The Church has surveyed that "wondrous cross," seen that "sacred head once wounded," and sung of its "debt augmented" which He paid with His blood.

THANKFULLY FOR ME

I have often passed in thought by the place called Calvary. Saul, recently anointed king of Israel, was bidden by Samuel to go home by way of Rachel's tomb. Standing there, that stalwart son of Benjamin would remember that Rachel died in giving birth to the father of his tribe. His life meant her death. At Calvary "we've adoring stood and gazed at that wondrous cross." He saved me; Himself He could not save.

None of us can stand there unaffected. He who steels his heart against that revelation must bear his iniquity. He, too, will cry when it is too late, "He saved others—my friends, my family, my wife, my children—me He cannot save now. I passed Him by. I abused my privileges." What a cry!

Then, too, the verse must be true of us who have thus stood thankfully at the cross. We, too, must save others, and can only do it as we do not save ourselves. We may save others by our preaching, our practice, and our prayers, by provocation and by pity. We can save wives and husbands, and preachers, and backsliders, and Gentiles and Jews. Yea, we can save ourselves and them that hear us (1 Tim. 4:16). Let us look a little more closely at these aspects of salvation for others.

SALVATION BY PREACHING

I am made all things to all men that I might by all means save some (see 1 Cor. 9:18-23; 1 Cor. 1:18).

We save others when, as sowers, we scatter the precious seed of the gospel by which people are saved (Lk. 8:12). Paul's preaching was not a profession; it was a passion. He was prepared to surrender personal liberties to bring others into liberty. He was all things to all men that he might by all means save some. His sanctified "mobility" was because of a consecrated motive.

SALVATION BY PRACTICE

For how knowest thou, O wife, whether thou shalt save thy husband? or how knowest thou, O man, whether thou shalt save thy wife? (1 Cor. 7:16).

If any obey not the word, they also may without the word be won by the conversation [behavior] *of the wives* (1 Pet. 3:1).

In the Corinthian passage the conversion of one parent was not to disrupt the family ties (see in contrast Ezra 10:18-19, 44; Neh. 13:23-30). A Christian conversion rather sanctifies the relationship. Children were not to be put away as unclean. If Christian practice was as it should be, the normal expectancy would be that God, who instituted families, would extend His grace in salvation to the other members. The light which He had brought was to shine to all that were in the house (Mt. 5:15).

SALVATION BY PRAYER

For I know that this shall turn to my salvation through your prayer (Phil. 1:19).

Ardent servants of God, pressing into dangerous places, need salvation by our prayers. Paul was sure the prayers of the Philippians would result in his salvation from Roman bonds and in a joyous reunion with the saints. In this regard, "More things are wrought by prayer than this world dreams of."

> The weary ones had rest, the sad had joy,
> And wondered how:
> A plowman, singing at his work, had prayed,
> "Lord, help them now."
> Away in foreign lands they wondered how
> Their simple word had power;
> The Christians, two or three at home,
> Had met to pray an hour.
> Yes, we are always wondering, wondering how
> Because we do not see
> Someone alone and far away
> On bended knee.

SALVATION BY PROVOCATION

If by any means I might provoke to [jealousy] them which are my flesh, and might save some of them (Rom. 11:14).

Paul would provoke, if he could, his brethren the Jews to jealousy, by showing that if their rejection by God could bring such blessing to the Gentiles, what could not their reception bring, not only to Gentiles, but to themselves. Prophets had foretold their future national blessing and dipped their brushes into all the colors of the rainbow when portraying it; Paul would woo them to the banner of Christ even now. And we today can make our Christianity such a radiant thing, such an infectious thing, that people will desire it more than silver or gold.

SALVATION BY PITY

And of some have compassion, making a difference: and others save with fear, pulling them out of the fire, hating even the garment spotted by the flesh (Jude 22-23; see also Jas. 5:19-20).

Backsliding brethren need to be saved. Lot needed to be saved by Abraham, although he was reaping what he had sown and had not been generous to his uncle. But when Abraham heard that his nephew was taken captive, he had compassion and rescued him. We often need, like Barnabas, to go looking for a Saul, when there is a danger that he might be shunted off onto a siding in Christian service, and because there is a job that he can do at home.

Thus we save others in these holy exercises of the soul.

Ourselves we cannot save, for he that loves his own life shall lose it. We cannot save ourselves that expenditure if others are to be rich; that toil if others are to rest for ever; that weakness if others are to be made strong; those tears if others are to have them wiped away and laugh in holy joy.

> When I am dying how glad I shall be
> That the lamp of my life has been blazed out for Thee.

THREE

The Miracles
of the Cross

In contrast to the miracles of Moses, Peter, and Paul, which were the divine authentication of their mission and diminished when it was established, the miracles of our Lord go on through His public life and cluster at the cross. Although there were no miracles *on* the cross, no divine hand raised to prevent Jesus' death, there were certainly miracles *around* the cross, full attestation by God to the superlative character of the work wrought out there. Christ's work there, as ever, was approved by mighty signs and wonders. These miracles not only accredit the redemption which is in Christ Jesus, but demonstrate its character and scope. They are rays of light cast on the facets of redemption.

The first is the "dumb darkness which wrapt His soul a space"—the price of redemption; the second is the rent veil, the purpose of redemption—to bring us to God; the third and fourth are the earthquake and the opened graves, the power of redemption, in fact, the product of it; the fifth is the undisturbed grave clothes, the proof of redemption;

the sixth is the resurrection of the saints, the pledge of redemption.

THE DARKNESS: THE PRICE OF REDEMPTION

Now from the sixth hour there was darkness over all the land unto the ninth hour (Mt. 27:45).

There was darkness at noonday, and for the space of three hours—a darkness like the darkness of Egypt which could be felt, a sudden settling down of midnight gloom. At Jesus' birth the darkness of night was turned to brightest glory; now the brightness of the day was miraculously turned to Stygian night.

Bishop Nicolson in his *Six Miracles of Calvary* reminds us that it could not have been an eclipse of the sun, for the darkness lasted too long; and because the Jews' Passover— taking place at that time—was celebrated at the time of the full moon, when an eclipse of the sun would be impossible. The same writer also points out that the enemies of the cross did not deny the knowledge of the miraculous darkness. There is no record of indignant denials when it was preached and when the Gospel of Matthew appeared. Celsus and other brilliant opponents of Christianity could not and did not oppose it.

It is not simply that the sun did

> ...in darkness hide
> And shut His glories in,
> When the Incarnate Maker died,
> For man His creature's sin. —*Isaac Watts*

It was darkness triumphing over light, when the penalty of sin was being borne and when it drew forth the orphan cry of Immanuel. Here was a *"horror of great darkness,"* before which Abram's is but a passing shadow (Gen.

15:12). There in the darkness the patriarch was assured of the redemption of his people and of his own death at a good old age. Here in the horror of darkness and distance, the Son of God was enduring the birthpangs of redemption and being cut off in the midst of His days.

It was God who was indicating by the darkness the awful price of redemption. It was God who shut off the seeing of the curious and the callous and the cruel, permitting no human eye to see the "superlative anguish" of His Son. These sufferings are not described by the Evangelists. The hour of Gethsemane, the hour when He contemplated the sin-bearing is told out in terms of sweat like blood falling to the ground. But the actuality, the compressed sufferings of these hours, are not described. Even God would turn His eyes away.

> The Holy One did hide His face,
> O Christ, 'twas hid from Thee:
> Dumb darkness wrapt Thy soul a space:
> The darkness due to me. —*Anne Ross Cousin*

That was the price of redemption.

THE RENDING OF THE VEIL: THE PURPOSE OF REDEMPTION

And behold, the veil of the temple was rent in twain from the top to the bottom (Mt. 27:51).

The rending of the veil was the end of "the Jews' monopoly of religion," the end of an earthly priesthood. As with the darkness, the same enemies, Jews and Gentiles, pay unwitting tribute to it, in the absence of any denials of the rending of the veil in the Jewish temple. We should not have read that *"a great company of the priests were obedient to the faith"* (Acts 6:7) if the miracle had been denied from the first by the custodians of religion in Israel.

It could not have been the result of the earthquake since the rest of the furnishings of the temple remained intact. The building itself was not injured. Nor could human hands have torn the heavy veil apart. It was rent from top to bottom (a veil estimated to be 60 feet in height); it was the work of God and not of men. It occurred at the time of the evening sacrifice when priests would be in the Holy Place and therefore spectators of the portentous event. What unhallowed presence would have been allowed within the sacred enclosure at such a time as that?

The fact was obvious. The veil, which barred the way for all but the high priest once a year, was suddenly rent at the moment of the expiring of the Son of God. Any of the priests might now look in and behold the mercy seat with the marks of the victim slain. And if the inner sanctum lay open, if the Holiest could be entered, then it did away with the necessity of the high priest or any of his subordinates.

There was now *"A new and living way...through the veil, that is to say, His flesh"* (Heb. 10:20). This is the divine commentary on the event. The veil was of fine twined linen, and curiously wrought with cherubim, in colors of blue, purple and scarlet. It hung from hooks of gold. It was typical of the One whose flesh was rent at Calvary, which opened up the way to God.

In the blue and red colors we see heaven and earth combining, God manifest in flesh. In the blending of these in the purple we see God's King as well as Israel's. As the hooks of gold upheld the veil, we see that His perfect life of righteousness is predicated on His deity. Had that humanity remained untorn, the barrier would still be there. But He was wounded, and His wounding for our transgressions opened the way to God.

The purpose of redemption is clear. He died to bring us to God. No intervening priests are needed now; no waiting for the Day of Atonement now. The way is open—open now—open for all. Let us draw near with true hearts in full assurance of faith. The gate is open wide.

THE EARTHQUAKE AND THE OPENED GRAVES: THE POWER OF REDEMPTION

And the earth did quake, and the rocks rent; and the graves were opened (Mt. 27:51-52).

In the third miracle we see the convulsions of nature in terms not of terror as at Sinai, but of triumph. Earthquakes are common in the long history of man's seismography, but in the precision of the miracle, like the falling walls of Jericho, lay the miraculous factor. The earthquake was also at the precise moment of our Lord's death.

These miracles are linked together in the sacred record. The quaking of the earth and the opening of the graves made the centurion and the soldiers fear greatly and say, *"Truly this was the Son of God"* (Mt. 27:54). Matthew alone records these phenomena, but his Gospel appears in the lifetime of the witnesses, and thereby he challenges any to deny it. There is no mention of denial of the miracles by hostile Jews living in the early days of the church, nor by later opponents such as Celsus, Porphry, and Julian.

The discriminate effect of the earthquake should be noted. The rocks rent but the crosses stood. Graves were opened, no doubt the result of the earthquake, but it was not a general opening of graves: it was a restricted thing. It was the graves of *saints* that were opened, with a view to their resurrection when Jesus arose. There was a divine intelligence, a supernatural discrimination in the uncovered tombs. The graves of the saints were ready to deliver, indeed, Hades itself must be ready to give up, at the shout of the Conqueror. Such is the power of redemption.

Here was a miniature picture of redemption as it will affect the whole company of the saints of God. It is a sample, a specimen of the life and immortality that has been brought to light through the gospel. Because of that death at Golgotha, the place of a skull, death will flee. Because of that redemption, we do not bury the bodies of the blessed dead, we sow them, in the certainty of a return in greater measure and beauty. It is sown in corruption; it is raised in incorruption. It is sown a natural body; it is raised a spiritual body (see 1 Cor. 15:42-44).

As it appears, it was only the graves of the saints that were affected that day. If others were, no fact of resurrection is noted. Now the scripture declares:

> *The hour is coming, in the which all that are in the graves shall hear His voice, and shall come forth; they that have done good, unto the resurrection of life; and they that have done evil, unto the resurrection of damnation"* (Jn. 5:28-29).

But the resurrection of the just has precedence, and it is to this that the designed and discerning resurrection of the saints points here. How exceeding is the greatness of God's power which can be seen toward us who believe! This power He wrought in Christ when He, who had bruised Him for our iniquities, raised Him from the dead and set Him at His own right hand in the heavens.

THE GRAVE CLOTHES: THE PROOF OF REDEMPTION

> *Then cometh Simon Peter following him, and went into the sepulcher and seeth the linen clothes lie, and the napkin, that was about His head, not lying with the linen clothes, but wrapped together in a place by itself. Then went in also that other disciple, which came first to the sepulcher, and he saw and believed* (Jn. 20:6-8).

Dr. A. T. Pierson and others have drawn attention to the

fact that the words of verse 7 indicate the original convolutions of the wrappings that had been about the head of our Lord. These wrappings were undisturbed. This was doubtlessly true of all the graveclothes. It was this that John perceived in coming into the tomb a little later. It is interesting to note the three words for *seeing* in the context. John came first and, standing outside, looked and saw *(blepo)* at a glance that the Lord was not in the tomb. In verse 6, Peter entered and saw *(theorei)*, a closer contemplation by reason of his proximity. In verse 8, John grasped the significance of the undisturbed graveclothes. He saw *(eiden)* and believed.

Here was proof enough for John and Peter, we may be sure. These external evidences would not motivate them as would the testimony of the Scriptures from the Lord's own lips as seen in Luke's account of the disciples on the way to Emmaus. Here we read,

> *For as yet they knew not the scripture, that He must rise again from*
> *the dead. Then the disciples went away again unto their own home*
> (Jn. 20:9-10).

But as a result of the ministry of the Scriptures, the disciples rose up the same hour and returned to Jerusalem to tell the disciples that their Lord was risen indeed. In the seven great witnesses of Christ's resurrection in 1 Corinthians 15 the Scriptures are placed first. Christ rose again according to the Scriptures (v. 4). Yet the undisturbed graveclothes were enough for John in the meantime. Later he would get a sight of Jesus Himself, would hear Him, handle Him, the Word of Life (1 Jn. 1:1).

If the Lord in rising again left the graveclothes behind Him, so shall we. If indeed that resurrection body had none of the apparent limitations that He had assumed in the days of His flesh so that He could now come into a room, the doors being fastened (Jn. 20:19), and vanish suddenly out of sight from the home at Emmaus (Lk. 24:31), then is this not a hint of the body in which we, too, shall glorify God and serve Him for ever? Here is the proof of resurrection indeed, of Christ's own people, and with what body they shall come. The Apostle Paul does not seem altogether to deplore the questions raised in 1 Corinthians 15:35: *"How are the dead raised up? And with what body do they come?"* since he proceeds to show by analogy and revelation the answers to these questions. We shall be fashioned like His own body of glory.

THE RESURRECTION OF SAINTS:
THE PLEDGE OF REDEMPTION

And many bodies of the saints which slept arose, and came out of their graves after His resurrection, and went into the holy city, and appeared unto many (Mt. 27:52-53).

The graves of the saints were ready to deliver; Hades must give up at the Conqueror's call, but the order of resurrection must be *"Christ the Firstfruits; afterward they that are Christ's at His coming"* (1 Cor. 15:23). If that "Corn of Wheat" falls into the ground and dies He cannot abide alone, but must bring forth much fruit. Many saints shall rise out of that death. If He arose, so shall we. All in Christ shall be made alive, even as all in Adam die. The triumph of the Son of God is the triumph of the sons of God.

Beloved, now are we the sons of God, and it doth not yet appear what we shall be: but we know that, when He shall appear, we shall be like Him; for we shall see Him as He is (1 Jn. 3:2).

FOUR

The Cries of the Cross:
Their Tenderness

The perfect ministry of the cross, in terms of divine communications, is seen in the seven utterances of our Lord. At a time when other sufferers might excusably have been given to morbid introspection and self-pity, these cries exhibit a breadth of interest, a depth of consecration, and a vigor of utterance that is profound because they are God breathed. Here is no waning of His power, whether mental or physical. His last cries will not be in the nature of a parting sigh, as we sometimes sing, and deplore that none were there to share it, but spoken in a loud voice that heaven as well as earth, and hell as well as heaven, might hear.

There is a world of sympathy in the first three cries:

- *Father, forgive them; for they know not what they do.*
- *Verily I say unto thee, To day shalt thou be with Me in paradise.*
- *Woman, Behold thy son!...Behold thy mother!*

There is a world of suffering in the next two:

• *My God, My God, Why hast Thou forsaken Me?*
• *I thirst.*

There is a world of satisfaction in the last two:

• *It is finished.*
• *Father, into Thy hands I commend My spirit.*

In the first three we have the tenderness of these divine communications; in the next two the tragedy of them; in the closing words we have the triumph of them.

In the first and last the Father is there; in the middle cry He is gone in the terrible distance and the terrible darkness that sin has made. In the first our holy Substitute is entering a greater gloom than Gethsemane; in the last He emerges from it. In both there is the consciousness and the comfort of the Father's presence. But in the middle cry there is utter forsakenness even by His God. This is the mystery of the cross to which we can only turn with unshod feet and broken hearts.

Drawing near with true hearts, let us see in the first three the tenderness of those cries.

THE FIRST MESSAGE

Then said Jesus, Father, forgive them, for they know not what they do (Lk. 23:34).

Note the provocation: *"**Then** said Jesus."* Against the *"when"* of verse 33 you have the *"then"* of verse 34. Against the dark background of human hate, Jesus our Lord painted the bright foreground of divine love. Against the scourging and the laceration and the gaping wounds, against the contusion and the dislocation and the tension and the congestion, against the thirst and the fever, against the taunts and the jibes and the sneers, you have the melting tenderness of a cry for forgiveness for the perpetrators of the ghastliest deed in the long history of human atrocities. By it the swift chariot wheels of the judgment of God might well be hindered. By it the portals of heaven were thrown open and access offered to the very murderers of the Son of God. By it hope is offered to the lowest and the greatest sinner outside of hell. By the act of dying our Lord made forgiveness a righteous act as well as merciful.

Note the prayer: *"Father, forgive them."* Our Saviour never at any time said, "Forgive Me." Every other man who has been on earth has needed forgiveness, of God or of his fellow. It is no mark of masculinity, much less of veracity, that any man declares he has never needed to plead for forgiveness. And no time is so propitious and so commonly used by recalcitrant transgressors as the hour of death. When the last sun is going down, memory is often active, and a truer perspective on personal conduct is granted, calling forth a desire for forgiveness from God and from men.

Yet here in the last hours of His life there is no cry from Jesus for forgiveness for Himself. It is not, "Forgive Me"; it is *"Forgive them."* Nor does our Lord exercise His divine prerogative and forgive sins Himself, though He had power on earth to forgive sins (Mt. 9:6). Now He is the victim, the substitute, the sin-bearer. Lifted up from the earth, He calls upon the Father in heaven to do so.

In some of its uses the word translated *"forgive"* bears the thought of forbearance rather than forgiveness. It is the word *"Suffer little children to come unto Me"* (Lk. 18:16). It is used in another scene at the cross when the enemies of Jesus said, *"Let be, let us see whether Elias will come to save Him"* (Mt. 27:49). It is the thought of prevention rather than pardon in view in these scriptures. Some have thought therefore that in the first cry our Lord was praying for the staying of the floodgates of Almighty wrath, until this people got the offer of forgiveness at Pentecost and repudiated their ignorance.

> *And now, brethren, I wot that through ignorance ye did it, as did also your rulers* (Acts 3:17).

Thus some would read the passage, *"Father, forbear, for they know not what they do."*

Yet the preponderance of the use of the word, as a concordance will show, is for forgiveness. *"And when ye pray... forgive"* (Lk. 11:2-4). *"So likewise shall My heavenly Father do also unto you, if ye from your hearts forgive not every one his brother their trespasses"* (Mt. 18:35). The first cry is on behalf of the murderers of Jesus, however careless, however culpable.

Note the plea: *"...For they know not what they do."* Not a plea that God will overlook the sin, but that He will forgive it. Much less that they were not really to blame. Here we have the culpability of ignorance. It was ever taught in Israel:

> *If a soul shall sin through ignorance...then let him bring for his sin ...a young bullock without blemish unto the Lord for a sin offering* (Lev. 4:2–3).
> *And if the whole congregation of Israel sin through ignorance...and are guilty...* (Lev. 4:13).
> *When a ruler hath sinned...and is guilty...* (Lev. 4:22).
> *And if any of the common people sin through ignorance...and be guilty...* (Lev. 4:27).

Thus whether priest, ruler, or common people sinned ignorantly, they were guilty and needed the blood of atonement. Around the place called Calvary, priest, ruler, and common people united in guilt, however ignorantly, and needed not only the plea of the outraged Victim, but the atoning blood which He shed.

Ignorance is not innocence. We acknowledge it continually in things of the State and of the street. We park our cars in wrong places and are ticketed for our negligence. Yet we never rush into court to plead innocence for ignorance. The law is there, the signs are there to indicate the restricted areas. We have ignored them. Yet in things spiritual and eternal we often mentally plead ignorance for sins of which we are truly guilty. With the Bible in our homes, the gospel in the air, and the Spirit of God in the world to convict, we are inexcusable indeed. Oh, the magnanimity, the generosity of that first cry of Christ which pleads for pardon while laying the ground upon which pardon must rest. *"We have redemption through His blood, even the forgiveness of sins"* (Col. 1:14).

THE SECOND MESSAGE

And Jesus said unto him, Verily I say unto thee, Today shalt thou be with Me in paradise (Lk. 23:43).

A dying thief would be the first trophy of redeeming grace that day. An outcast, a felon, a man with tainted past and tarnished name, a man with a broken body and a blasphemous mouth, will walk by the side of Jesus in the paradise of God. A man who spent his last evening in the gloom of a dungeon on earth will spend his first morning in the "Garden of Delights" in heaven. This is liberality in the superlative degree:

Where sin abounded, grace did much more abound (Rom. 5:20).

The character of his faith. We do not know of a man who seemed to get such an insight into divine things in such a short time as the man whom we commonly call the dying thief. He got a grasp of real values in the spiritual realm in his remaining hours of life, an understanding that many do not secure in a lifetime. We do not know one who used his last opportunity to better advantage than he. Considering that he joined his fellow malefactor at first in taunting and vilification (Mt. 27:44; Mk. 15:32), his sudden disavowal and discernment can only be explained as all true conversions are explained, by the same abounding grace of God where sin had flourished.

His faith was intelligent. It was not based on the miracles of the cross, for up till now there had been none. It was not an ignorant, superstitious thing. He had a clear grasp of the fundamentals of theology and confessed them. He was no atheist, for he expressed a fear of falling into the hands of the living God. He had no false notions of his own guilt or of the justice of his punishment. *"We receive,"* said he, *"the due reward of our deeds"* (Lk. 23:41).

He confessed the sinlessness of Jesus. *"This Man hath done nothing amiss."* He intimated his faith in resurrection. *"Lord, remember me when Thou comest in Thy kingdom"* (Lk. 23:42). But how could the Sufferer on the middle cross remember him if He were going to die Himself that day and never be raised again? He declared his convictions in Christ's coming kingdom, and therefore in the legitimacy of His claims. *"Remember me when Thou comest in Thy kingdom."* It was as if he had said, "Lord, Thou are crowned with thorns today, but I believe Thou shalt one day have a diadem of glory. Men bow the knee in derision today; one day they shall bow in worship and fear. Remember me when Thou comest in Thy kingdom."

God wants our faith to be intelligent; not the superstitious thing of the heathen, or the baseless, traditional thing of the pseudo-Christian religions of men, but a living, vocal thing based on the final revelation of the Word of God concerning Jesus Christ our Lord. God does not ask for mere credulity. He always gives us something credible, something sound. We, too, must see our guilt and confess it, and see the guiltlessness of the One who hung on the middle cross for us. Our faith must be in resurrection,

If thou shalt confess with thy mouth the Lord Jesus, and shalt believe in thine heart that God hath raised Him from the dead, thou shalt be saved (Rom. 10:9).

His faith was humble. Compare his humble prayer and the Lord's gracious answer. The thief got infinitely more than he could ask or think. He asked for a thought and got a presence. He asked for a thought in the future, and got the present possession of the companionship of Christ. He asked for a thought in the future kingdom on earth, and got the blessed assurance of walking that day with Christ in paradise.

Again we say, Oh, the magnanimity of the cross!

> *Now unto Him who is able*
> > *who is able to do exceeding abundantly*
> > > *exceeding abundantly above all*
> > > > *above all that we ask*
> > *or think,*
> > *according to the power that worketh in us.*
> *Unto Him be glory in the church,*
> > *by Jesus Christ,*
> > > *throughout all ages,*
> > > > *world without end.*
> > > > > *Amen* (Eph. 3:20–21).

The courage of his faith. Do not despise the man because he came at the eleventh hour. Jesus did not. We know nothing of the man's privileges and opportunities before this. Think, rather, of the splendid courage in the face of such fearful odds. His confession was not only for the ears of the other thief and of the Lord Himself; it was for the crowd. It was for the chief priests and rulers and scribes and Pharisees who must have scowled and snarled when he uttered it. *"This Man hath done nothing amiss."* (Lk. 23:41). He thereby condemned the wicked hands which had crucified the Son of God. He thereby cut himself off from any favors which they might have given him when he joined at first in their revilings. Now he condemns them. They have crucified an innocent Man, in fact, the King who one day shall sit on the holy hill of Zion (Ps. 2:6).

His faith was not the secret faith of a Joseph of Arimathea, but an articulate, active, aggressive thing. He dared to take a stand for Jesus in the face of a howling mob cursing and clamoring for His life. What joy it must have brought to our divine Lord! Already He was tasting something of the joy set before Him who would endure the cross and despise the shame. How quick He was to reward this courageous confession, super-abounding in His reply.

The challenge of his faith. Do not deplore the shortness of the time the converted thief had for testimony for Christ. He used it to wonderful advantage. If you can use your last moments of life to as good an end, you may press into a minute the virtues of a lifetime. If you can take a stand for Jesus Christ when all around you are blaspheming that worthy Name, you may have restored in a short time years that the locusts have eaten. If you can be articulate when around you there are others who secretly believe on Him but are silent for fear and because they love the praise of men more than the praise of God, you may redeem the time of which evil days have robbed you. Oh, to take a more vigorous, vital, vocal stand for our rejected Lord!

The dying thief challenges us to an intelligent, humble, courageous faith. This second message shows the speedy response which Grace Incarnate makes when a man from the lowest ranks of earth confessed His name before hostile men.

A thief will pass through the serried ranks of angels and sit with Christ in the paradise of God, for He promised:

Whosoever therefore shall confess Me before men, him will I confess also before My Father which is in heaven (Mt. 10:32).

THE THIRD MESSAGE

When Jesus therefore saw His mother, and the disciple standing by, whom He loved, He saith to His mother, 'Woman, behold thy son.' Then saith He to the disciple, 'Behold thy mother.' And from that hour that disciple took her unto his own... (Jn. 19:26-27).

A heart-warming contrast in attitude is seen in the little company of followers that stood near the cross. It was composed of a few devout women and John the disciple. Among them, and probably most affected of all, was Mary the mother of Jesus. Our Lord's third word from the cross was directed to her and to John. The first cry was on behalf of the rabble crowd clamoring for His death; the second was for the felon by His side; the third in this trilogy of magnanimity was on behalf of His mother and of John.

She who gave her breast for the infant head to rest on will have an arm to lean on in the days to come, and the man chosen to bear her will be one who leaned on Jesus' breast at supper. The breast of Mary! The breast of Jesus! The breast of John, for he will take her, not simply to his home, but to all that he has. There is no word for *"home"* in the original. It is too limited a thought here. It was to his own, to all that he had, to his heart as well as to his home that he took Mary. Many a woman has a room in the house of her son, but not in the heart of his family. The Apostle of Love would take Mary to all that he could give.

El-Shaddai, translated "the Almighty" in the Old Testament, in the opinion of many is literally, "the Breasted One," from *shad,* the female breast; and draws attention to the ability of God to shield and to succor His people at all times. John later would write of the Man on the middle cross and call Him *"Alpha and Omega,"* coequal with the Almighty of the Old Testament (Rev. 1:8-11; 22:13-14). He was sufficient for the need of His own then; He is sufficient today.

Why was not Mary put in the care of one of her other sons or daughters? (Mt. 13:55-56). She was probably a widow by this time since Joseph seems to disappear and Mary is given into the care of another. But why not to her own children? Is it not because they were up till now unbelievers? (Jn. 7:3-5). Later, after Christ's resurrection, they would be numbered among the disciples (Acts 1:14). Our Lord recognizes the deeper spiritual tie. He had already repudiated the mere earthly relationship as establishing any prior claim upon Him (Mt. 12:46-50; 2 Cor. 5:16).

It is true that Jesus would leave us an example that we should follow His steps:

> *If a man provide not for his own...he hath denied the faith, and is worse than an infidel* (1 Tim. 5:8).

Though our Lord was on the cross to meet the deeper need of our souls, including Mary's, He would not forget her temporal need. His chivalrous manhood could do no less.

1. "Woman," A revelation of life. It was the *"Seed of the woman"* who would bruise the head of the serpent (Gen. 3:15). The Son of God came of a woman (Gal. 4:4). The term doubtless drew attention in the beginning to the virgin birth. Not that the phrase *"the seed of the woman"* is conclusive of this, for see Genesis 16:10—Hagar's seed; and Revelation 12:17—the woman's seed. The Roman Catholic Church claims the woman of verse 1 of that chapter to be Mary, exalted and Queen of heaven, but what does it do with the phrase at the end of the chapter, *"the remnant of her seed"* (Rev. 12:17), while supporting the dogma that Mary had no more children after Jesus? The woman of verse 1 is of course Israel, of whom, according to the flesh, Christ came. He was the true seed of the woman. Seed is masculine, but Joseph was not the father of Jesus. It is noteworthy that when we have the first sin in the world, we have not only the promise of a Sin-Purger but a suggestion of the miracle of His advent (Gen. 3:15).

When the fullness of the time was come, God sent forth His Son, made of a woman...to redeem... (Gal. 4:4-5).

Here was the woman and there was her Seed. The bruising of the head of the serpent would follow. Life had come to end death.

2. "Woman," a revelation of light. It is not "my mother" nor even "mother" but *"woman."* It is never "mother" when Jesus was speaking to Mary in the New Testament. Never! We do not say He never used the term. It is boyhood's dearest word. But none of the evangelists record that He used it. He would not countenance a word which could give the slightest support in the years to come for Mariolatry, the worship of Mary. The Faithful Witness would deliver souls from such blasphemy.

Matthew records that when the wise men came they saw the young child with Mary His mother, they fell down and worshiped Him (not them) and presented to Him (not them) gifts: gold, frankincense, and myrrh. They were wise men, the seers and sages and scientists of the day. If Mary is to be worshiped, here was the golden opportunity to do so. But they knew better than to worship Mary.

Luke will record that Mary, instead of calling herself the mother of God, instead glorified God her Saviour (Lk. 1:46-47). Mary knew better. Luke will also note that when Jesus was born Mary brought her sin offering, as all Jewish women did at the birth of a child (see Lev. 12:6; Lk. 2:24). He will also draw attention to the fact that the angel Gabriel, and Mary's cousin Elisabeth, speaking by the Holy Spirit, will both call Mary blessed (happy) *among* women, but not blessed *above* them (Lk. 1:28, 42). The last view of Mary in the Bible and on earth shows her praying with (not for) the disciples (Acts 1:14).

Christ's humanity was the limit of Mary's motherhood toward Him. Note the prophecy of Isaiah 9:6. The child was born, the Son was given. God gave the Son; Mary mothered the child. He was made of the seed of David, but declared the Son of God with power (Rom. 1:4). Here in our Lord's use of *"woman"* is a revelation of omniscience, a revelation of light. Mary is not the Queen of Heaven or the Mother of God, as far as the declarations of the Son of God are concerned, nor of the revelations given to any of the apostles, including Peter. The title *"woman"* shows Christ ratifying that repudiation of the earthly relationship which He had made before (Mt. 12:46-50). It was now complete. John was now her son; she was his mother. Any person, even the dying thief, is as close as Mary in the realm of grace.

3. "Woman," a revelation of love. We are sure that there must have been a tenderness in our Lord's use of the word that cannot be reproduced. It would pierce His heart as it must have pierced Mary's. Yet He must tread this path alone, and her tears would be wiped away with the discovery that the Saviourhood of Christ meant more to her than the earthly sonship ever could. Our Lord's familiar use of the word *"woman"* in addressing Mary would shield her from any insult and injury to which she might have been exposed in that hour. He would spare her that. There was love, as well as light and life, in Jesus' use of *"woman."*

"Woman, behold thy son!...behold thy mother!" (Jn. 19:26-27). Surely this was the time for love to exalt Mary above all created beings; this was the time for superlative titles and mediatorial honors, if Mary is to be exalted. But they are lacking here. The Lawgiver is honoring His own commandments. He will honor His mother, which must include providing for her if she needed that. It cannot be, as Rome asserts, that Mary is put in charge of John, for then the record would have read that from that hour Mary took John unto her own. No! It is Mary put under the care of John, and John put in charge of Mary. From that hour the beloved disciple took her to his heart and home.

It is a great privilege to be given an assignment by a great person. Inasmuch as we do it to one of the least of His own, we serve the Lord Christ (Mt. 25:40). We do not know if John needed a mother to care for him, but he certainly needed a mother to care for. This word from the cross was not only forethought for Mary's support; it was foresight for John's success. Every task given to us by the Lord is the necessary preparation for the work of the future. Continual exercises in self-sacrifice are always in the highest interest of the soul.

What conversations John and Mary would have in the years to come. Tradition says they enjoyed some twelve years together. Those quiet years at Nazareth, about which we know so little (and which are not enriched by the Apocryphal Gospels of Rome wherein miracles are supposedly wrought capriciously by the boy Jesus) would often be the subject of conversation in John's home. While he might conceivably have known much of those years, and while John's future subject in the Gospels would not deal with those scenes, yet there would be much to enrich his own life in the account of the early life of his Lord.

John's was to be the task that Christ would have done. Our assignment is similar in that we represent Christ in His absence. What work He has to do He would do by us. We are the Johns of the dispensation. Christ has no hands but our hands; no tongue but ours; no feet but our feet. Wherever one is doing the will of the Father in heaven and needs a home, the same is our Lord's mother and brethren and sisters. There you have an assignment for a disciple who loves the Lord.

> *And those members of the body which we think to be less honorable, upon these we bestow more abundant honor* (1 Cor. 12:23).

If Christ in the weakness of the cross cared for His own, what will He not do today in the plenitude of His power and resources on the throne?

FIVE

The Cries of the Cross: Their Tragedy

My God, My God, why hast Thou forsaken Me?
MARK 15:34

THE FOURTH MESSAGE

Here is where we tread, if we tread at all, with unshod feet. Here is where we must beware of sacrilegious curiosity and unholy intrusion. We seem to hear our Lord say afresh, *"Whither I go, thou canst not follow Me now"* (Jn. 13:36). We borrow the words of another as he approached the same subject:

> At the commencement of this study I would place on record, not idly and not for mere sake of doing so, but under the urgency of a great conviction, that I am deeply conscious of approaching things too high, and too profound for any finality of statement.
> —G. Campbell Morgan: *The Crises of the Christ*

These words of Christ were spoken at the end of the three hours of darkness. About these hours nothing is said.

Human lips, however profane, however pitiful, must have been sealed in the terror and intensity of that darkness. Perhaps the only sounds heard were the groanings and the gasps of the thieves, and the splash of the drops of blood as they fell and gathered at the foot of the crosses. Human eyes, however curious, however callous, were not permitted to view the supreme agonies of the Son of God. And so no one can tell us about them. All we can gather is from the cries that escaped the lips of the Substitute at the close of the darkness.

Of the destination of the sin-offering on the great day of Israel's atonement, God said, *"Unto a land not inhabited"* (Lev. 16:22). From the sixth to the ninth hour on the cross our Sin-Offering was in a land not inhabited. Even God was not to be found. *"My God, My God, why hast Thou forsaken Me?"* (Mt. 27:46). That forsakenness was the end of the road in the Shepherd's search for the sheep. Truly,

> None of the ransomed ever knew
> How deep were the waters crossed,
> Nor how dark was the night that the Lord passed through
> E'er He found the sheep that was lost.   *—Elizabeth C. Clephane*

If God's *day* of grace is as *a thousand years*, there is an *eternity* of suffering in the compressed *three hours* of the darkness of the cross.

In the daylight we see our Lord's suffering at the hands of men; in the darkness He suffered at the hands of God. In the former it is the injustice of men; in the latter it is the justice of God. It is man's hatred of the Bearer of sin; it is God's hatred of the burden of sin.

Because of the orphan cry of Psalm 22, I have the companionship of Psalm 23. Because he *"wanted"* in Psalm 22, I shall not want in Psalm 23. Because He cried, *"My God, My God, why hast Thou forsaken Me?"* I cry, *"The*

Lord is my Shepherd." Because He really died, there is left for me but the valley of the "shadow" of death, where I fear no evil.

This is the middle cry of the cross, and the middle word of that cry is *"Why?"* All of us have used it in our anguish and in our perplexity.

1. We do not comprehend the "why" of our Saviour's cry because the measure of it is the measure of our guilt. We do not understand it because we do not understand sin—its character, its defilement, its enormity, its culpability.

2. We do not comprehend that "why" because we do not understand holiness. The answer to it is given in the psalm from which the cry is quoted. *"But Thou art holy"* (Ps. 22:3). David could never really know the profound depths of the words with which he began his complaint. It may be questioned whether any living man has ever been forsaken of God. That is the full harvest of sin, the issue of it. If while the lamp of life holds on to burn, and the greatest sinner may return, then none can really be forsaken of God in this life. David said,

I have been young, and now am old; yet have I not seen the righteous forsaken, nor his seed begging bread" (Ps. 37:25).

A thousand years will have to roll by before the Righteous One will be forsaken, even by His God. It is reserved for One only, the Mediator between God and men, to be forsaken. *"Persecuted, but not forsaken,"* (2 Cor. 4:9) was Paul's comfort—and ours—his buoy amid the billows.

At my first answer [defense] *no man stood with me, but all...forsook me...Notwithstanding the Lord stood with me"* (2 Tim. 4:16-17).

The Lord did not forsake His tried and lonely servant, if

men did, but on the cross in the middle cry of anguish, we reach the depths of abandonment. And we cannot comprehend it, because we do not understand unapproachable holiness, outraged holiness, vindicated holiness.

3. We do not comprehend that *"why"* because we do not really understand love and grace and salvation. It will take all the ages to come to show the exceeding riches of God's grace in His kindness toward us through Christ Jesus (Eph. 2:7). If we could grasp the depths of the riches, both of the wisdom and knowledge of God; if we could search His judgments and find out His ways; if we could know the mind of the Lord and be His counselor (Rom. 11:33-34), we might well begin to understand that *"why."* As in nature the depths of certain waters are determined by the height of the mountains that rise sheer above them, so we can never understand the depths because we cannot attain to the heights.

The middle cry of the cross leaves us alone and on our faces in the presence of God.

Therefore I was left alone, and saw this great vision, and there remained no strength in me: for my comeliness was turned in me into corruption, and I retained no strength. Yet heard I the voice of His words: and when I heard the voice of His words, then was I in a deep sleep on my face, and my face toward the ground (Dan. 10:8-9).

In Deuteronomy 21:18-23 there is the solemn law of the rebellious son. When the point was reached that his father and mother felt they could no longer go on with his stubbornness and rebellion, the son was to be brought to the elders of the city and stoned to death. If hung on a tree as a spectacle to all that passed by, his body was not to remain all night, but was to be buried that day. One of the remarkable things of the Old Testament revelation is that there is no instance of that law ever being carried out. Every father spared his own son as far as we read. Even Absalom, rebellious son of David, is not given up to stoning at the command of his father. *"Deal gently for my sake with the young man, even with Absalom,"* (2 Sam. 18:5) David pleads to the captains of his army who are setting out to meet the forces of his rebel son. If he hangs on a tree later, it will not be his father's hand that will accomplish it. If he lies under a heap of stones, it will be because one of the captains, Joab, heeded not the commands of his king.

Turning to the pages of the New Testament, we are asked at once to behold an obedient Son. *"This is My beloved Son,"* says the Father, *"in whom I am well pleased"* (Mt. 3:17). But look again and you will see Him on a tree. God spared not His own Son, but delivered Him up for us all (Rom. 8:32). Every father in the Old Testament spared his son. The heart of the New Testament revelation is that He who could have spared His Son, the only One who ever perfectly and continuously obeyed Him, spared Him not. That is what puts us prostrate before the cross.

Let us look again at the text and notice the period, the power, and the price of that utterance that brought us the comfort of the words of Hebrews 13:5,

> *He hath said, I will never, [no never,] leave thee, nor forsake thee.*

THE PERIOD

It was the ninth hour (Mt. 27:46), the hour of the evening sacrifice. The morning sacrifice was at the third hour; our nine o'clock in the forenoon. The evening sacrifice was the ninth hour; three in the afternoon. Turning back the pages of Holy Writ, we grasp something of the significance of the moment.

1. 1 Kings 18:36. Elijah was not forsaken when in splendid isolation he stood against the thousands of Israel and the 450 prophets of Baal. It was on Mount Carmel, meaning "the garden of God," so-called because of its verdure, its trees and flowers and grasses, lovelier than any place in the region; Mount Carmel whose foot dipped the waters of the Mediterranean, from whose summit a glorious view of the sea was obtained.

In the early morning the crowds converged on the high place to gain a vantage point for the contest between the worshippers of Baal, the sun-god, and Jehovah, the God of Israel. The marshalled feet of the prophets of Baal could be heard and presently they were seen in their glittering robes, with the sun-symbols flashing on their brows. Then the litter arrived carrying the king, Ahab.

The crowd stood still as Elijah spoke. *"How long halt ye between two opinions?"* They answered him *"not a word."* (1 Ki. 18:21). He challenged the people: let the God that answered by fire be the God. Baal was the lord of the sun; let him prove it now. Jehovah had answered by fire at the burning bush; in the pillar by night; at the top of Sinai, on the murmurers in Israel. Let Him do it again. What a scene!

First the prophets of Baal had their turn. *"O Baal, hear us"* (1 Ki. 18:26), they chanted in monotonous monosyllables as they marched round and round their altar. But Baal did not hear, and they grew frenzied and fierce and fearful, and leaped upon their altar. The sun, their god, climbed higher in the heavens, until he ascended his throne at noon. But Baal did not hear; the sun's fierce rays on the upturned faces of the priests was the only burning they received.

Then Elijah waxed sarcastic (1 Ki. 18:27–28):

> *Cry aloud, for he is a god; either he is talking or he is pursuing, or*
> *he is on a journey, or peradventure he sleepeth, and must be awak-*

ened. And they cried aloud and cut themselves after their manner with knives and lancets, till the blood gushed out upon them.

The whole was guaranteed to touch the heart of any heathen deity. Baal should have heard if he were there. But he was not there; it was all a delusion and a show. Baal had forsaken them, and three more hours pass until the sun begins to decline in the west. Their chance was past; their altar was cold and smokeless, the bullock unconsumed.

And now that lone man comes forward. It is the time of the offering of the evening sacrifice; the ninth hour. The Man of God gathered twelve stones, symbol of the unity of Israel in the sight of God, made a trench round about the altar which he filled with water, cut the bullock in pieces and laid them upon the wood he had placed carefully on the altar. Then he called upon Jehovah.

Hear me, O Lord, hear me, that this people may know that Thou art the Lord God, and that Thou hast turned their heart back again. Then the fire of the Lord fell and consumed the burnt sacrifice, and the wood, and the stones and the dust, and licked up the water that was in the trench (1 Ki. 18:37-38).

At the ninth hour, Jehovah heard. The heathen were slain and there was a sound of abundance of rain. At that very moment Elijah seemed to hear the hurrying feet of the clouds gathered to drench the land with refreshing rain.

Elijah was heard at the ninth hour. Heaven had answered him then. But here is heaven's Man of God, and at the ninth hour Jesus cried,

My God, My God, why hast Thou forsaken Me? (Mt. 27:46).

Baal had forsaken his own, but behold, O heavens, and see the Righteous forsaken by the true God.

But look again, more closely still, and you will see, not the fire consuming the sacrifice, but the sacrifice consuming the fire of judgment. Later the fire of Pentecost will fall; the showers of Pentecostal blessing will fall upon the waiting people. And as the people of old shouted, *"The Lord, He is the God,"* (1 Ki. 18:39) shall we not, beside that sacrifice of Mount Calvary, say, with bursting hearts like Thomas, *"My Lord and my God"* (Jn. 20:28).

2. Daniel 9:21. Daniel was not forsaken when toward the close of his long life he understood that the time was drawing near for the deliverance of Israel. Jeremiah had prophesied it, and Daniel set his heart to pray to God as if his prayer alone were the predetermined cause of that deliverance. He was a man of purity, of purpose, of prayer, of prophetic vision. The secret of the Lord was with him, because he feared Him. He discovered that all who will live godly shall suffer persecution, and he went down into the den of lions for his faithfulness to God.

While he was setting his heart to seek the Lord by prayer and supplication, by sackcloth and ashes, while he pleaded and cast his people before God, about the time of the evening oblation, Gabriel appeared and brought him, not a message of deliverance from the captivity of an earthly king, but of a Redeemer who would make an end of sins and bring in everlasting righteousness.

But nearly 500 years later, at the time of the evening oblation, there cried One purer than Daniel, more prayerful, more single in purpose, more profound in wisdom, more keen in prophetic vision, who suffered more for righteousness' sake—and His cry was one of utter forsakenness. *"My God, My God, why hast Thou forsaken Me?"*

> Oh, He's stronger than the strongest,
> He's far better than the best;
> And His love has lasted longest:
> It has stood the hardest test.

3. Ezra 9:5. Ezra was not forsaken when he cried to God at the time of the evening sacrifice. He was a ready scribe in the law of God, and had made a noble resolve, a sanctified New Year's Day resolution, as he turned his back on the glitter and glamor of Babylon to seek the law of the Lord, to do it, and to teach it in Israel.

And at the evening sacrifice I rose up from my heaviness, and having rent my garment and my mantle, I fell upon my knees, and spread out my hands unto the Lord, my God.

Ezra's powerful pleading wrought conviction in the hearts of the people and he was rewarded in seeing them turn from their unequal yokes to serve the living and true God.

4. Acts 3:1. After that battling, baffled cry from the cross, Peter would be heard at the ninth hour when he called on the power of the name of Jesus of Nazareth to heal the lame man. It is a story of contrasts. The hideous form of the man lame from the womb is set against the carving of the Beautiful Gate of the temple. The outward poverty of Peter is sharply in contrast to the inward wealth of his hold upon God; the beggar's poor request is in contrast to the rich answer of the servants of the Lord. The man who daily was laid at the gate to ask alms of those favored to enter in, is manifestly unlike the man walking and leaping and praising God, and entering with the worshippers into the courts of God.

5. Acts 10:3-4. Cornelius, a Gentile, would not be forsaken, his prayers and alms coming up for a memorial before God, at the ninth hour of the day. Like all the centurions of the New Testament, God makes him an object of grace and distinguishes him in some way among men.

These men were leaders of a hundred tough, fighting Roman soldiers, but *"out of the eater came forth meat, and out of the strong came forth sweetness"* (Jud. 14:14). The centurion who besought our Lord to heal his servant was great in his confidence. *"Speak the word only,"* said he, *"and my servant shall be healed"* (Mt. 8:8). The centurion at the cross was great in his confession. *"Certainly this was a righteous man;* (Lk. 23:47); *Truly this was the Son of God"* (Mt. 27:54). Cornelius was great in character, an exemplary man in every way. Yet he needed to be saved (Acts 11:13-14). The centurion in charge of Paul on the journey to Rome, was great in compassion, as seen in Acts 27:3, 43. Cornelius found at the ninth hour that God was the God of the Gentiles also. His prayer was heard.

So we who were afar off are brought nigh to God (Eph. 2:13). All is secured because of Him who was forsaken at that hour. The period was a moment heavy with portentous happenings and impending blessings.

THE POWER

"Jesus cried with a loud voice." There was no waning of the powers of Jesus our Lord. Like the Passover Lamb, a male of the first year, He died in the fullness of His strength. When we read that He gave up the ghost it means that He dismissed His spirit. Poets will write of His parting sigh and whispered prayer, but they have no place in the divine record. The remaining cries of Christ are of victory. Even the fifth word as we shall see, was not spoken that His thirst might be relieved, but that the Scriptures might be fulfilled. Thereafter, as with the fourth, His words will be uttered in a loud voice.

THE PRICE

Forsaken of God! Hell is where God is not to be found;

not to be seen. *"From Thy face shall I be hid"* (Gen. 4:14), wailed Cain. The impenitent shall be punished with everlasting destruction from the face of the Lord (2 Thess. 1:9, RV). The price of our nearness was His distance. The price of our forgiveness was His forsakenness. The price of the intimacy of the Father's face was the turning of the back of His God. Because of the affliction in that compressed eternity on the cross,

> *Our light affliction, which is but for a moment, worketh for us a far more exceeding and eternal weight of glory* (2 Cor. 4:17).

THE FIFTH MESSAGE

> *After this, Jesus knowing that all things were now accomplished, that the Scripture might be fulfilled, saith, I thirst* (Jn. 19:28).

1. The Deity of Christ. *"Jesus knowing...."* The Gospel of John is the Gospel of the knowingness, the omniscience of Christ. From chapter 1, verse 48 where Nathaniel says, *"Whence knowest Thou me?"* until the last chapter when Peter cries, *"Lord, Thou knowest all things"* (Jn. 21:17), John, who lay on Jesus' breast, is given the task of writing about the all-knowingness of Jesus our Lord. John is ever compressing infinity into finite terms.

> *Jesus knowing that the Father had given all things into His hands, and that He was come from God and went to God, He riseth from supper, and laid aside His garments, and took a towel and girded Himself* (Jn. 13:3-4).

In this sentence there is veiled all the story of the Incarnation. Here the omniscient One is also the omnipotent One into whose hands the Father had given all things. As well, He is the omnipresent One who was come from God and went to God. Laying aside His garments of glory and taking the towel, symbol of the bondservant, He stooped to wash away the stains of sin and of self from His own.

Jesus knowing that all things were now accomplished... (Jn. 19:28).

Many in deepest sympathy with the physical sufferings of Jesus have expatiated on His extreme thirst under the blaze of the eastern sun and in the anguish of His wounding, and have missed the dignity of this utterance. While our hearts would melt at the remembrance of His affliction and His misery, *"the wormwood and the gall"* (Lam. 3:19), and our souls be humbled within us, yet in keeping with the vigor of the fourth cry, is the dignity and intelligence of the fifth. Our Lord was in full possession of His mental faculties. No stupefying potion would He drink, though in fulfillment of Scripture He would let it touch His lips.

2. The Devotion of Christ. *"That the Scripture might be fulfilled."* If the first three cries of the cross are on behalf of other people, this one is on behalf of the Scriptures. Here again we perceive the intellectual vigor and spiritual devotion of our Lord. Now that He had emerged from the darkness and the distance, His mind was on the whole prophetic word. In God's law did He meditate day and night (Ps. 1:2). Scripture after scripture had been fulfilled. To Him had all the prophets witnessed, and His sufferings were the heart of their testimony. The betrayal, the price of it, the *"familiar friend"* who perpetrated it, the arrest, the arraignment, the scourging, the scorn, numbered with the transgressors, smitten of God—all had been fulfilled.

Yet there was one prophecy about the thirst of the Sufferer which had not yet taken place:

They gave Me gall for My [food], and in My thirst they gave me vinegar to drink" (Ps. 69:21).

Jesus..that the Scripture might be fulfilled saith, I thirst (Jn. 19:28).

It was not the thirst that opened the lips of the Son of God; it was the Scriptures. We must look beyond the human agony, beyond the *"strength dried up like a potsherd and [the] tongue cleaving to [the] jaws"* (Ps. 22:15), and see the inner revelation of a great devotion and try to catch something of its spell for our lives today. His thought at that crucial hour was for the completion of the Word of God. His words were not so much an appeal; they were an appointment, an application. The sacred word must needs be fulfilled. What devotion indeed! And we must assiduously see that the Scriptures are fulfilled in us; that we adorn its doctrine (beautify the teaching) of God our Saviour. We must search it to fulfill it, even in the midst of our afflictions.

3. The Dependence of Christ. *"I thirst."* The twelve legions of angels which He could have summoned at a moment were not commanded to come to His aid at the place called Calvary. Any one of them would have been highly honored to have brought Him a drink of the well that was by the gate of Bethlehem. But none was asked, and the men who might have succored Him brought Him vinegar.

The Lord of glory asked for water. The Maker of the world cried, *"I thirst."* How real His humanity. This verse that tells us of His essential deity, tells of His absolute humanity. Great is the mystery of godliness. God was manifest in flesh. The first revolt of the human mind in the early days of Christianity appears not to have been in the realm of Christ's claim to deity, but in the realm of His manifestation in humanity. Before the coming of Christ the heathen in Babylon (Dan. 2) could not conceive of deity taking on humanity. The wise men of Nebuchadnezzar told the king that the answer to his demand that they tell him not only the meaning of the dream, but the dream itself which he had forgotten, lay with the gods whose dwelling was not with flesh (Dan. 2:10). But after the coming of Jesus, the heathen at Lystra could conceive it, and erroneously thought that in Paul and Barnabas the gods had come down in the likeness of men (see Acts 14). After the mystery of godliness had become a fact, even the heathen rose to the possibility of it.

He who began His public ministry by hungering, ended it by thirsting. How real His humanity, again we say, His dependence. He needed food and rest. He did not annihilate distance by supernatural means, by a demonstration of deity, until after His resurrection, but was wearied ofttimes with His journey, sat down to rest, perhaps on a well, and asked for a drink.

In all things it behoved Him to be made like unto His brethren (Heb. 2:17).

In all our afflictions He was afflicted, and is therefore able to succor those that are tempted and tried.

Physically, our Lord's thirst is over. He will never thirst again. He waits to take His people to a place where they shall hunger no more, nor thirst. Vicariously, however, He still thirsts.

Then shall the righteous answer Him, saying, Lord, when saw we Thee an hungered and fed Thee, or thirsty and gave Thee drink?...And the King shall answer and say unto them, Verily, I say unto you, Inasmuch as ye have done it unto one of the least of these My brethren, ye have done it unto Me (Mt. 25:37, 40).

We can quench the thirst of our Lord when we give as little as a cup of water to a thirsty soul. And we can show our devotion to Him by our hungering and thirsting after righteousness: thirsting for the fulfillment of the precepts of Scripture in us.

SIX

The Cries of the Cross: Their Triumph

As we have indicated, if there is a world of sympathy in the first three cries of our Lord, and a world of suffering in the fourth and fifth, there is a world of satisfaction in these last two utterances of the cross.

THE SIXTH MESSAGE

It is finished (Jn. 19:30).

More has probably been written about the sixth cry than about all the others put together. Men have apprehended that there is more in this single utterance of Christ than can be understood, and they come again and again to try and plumb the depth of it. Eternity alone will suffice to comprehend the breadth and length, the depth and height of this mighty shout of triumph.

We read that Peter came into the high priest's palace to *"see the end"* (Mt. 26:58). He little realized the stupendous work that would be consumated before another day had ended. Calvary was *"the end of all flesh"* in that the full measure of man's probation would be at an end (Gen. 6:13). He who believed not was condemned already. Now was the judgment of the world.

Calvary was *"the end of the world"* when Christ had appeared to put away sin (Heb. 9:26). It was *"the end of the law for righteousness to every one that believeth,"* for by Christ's death the law would be satisfied (Rom. 10:4). It would be *"an end of sin"* that Daniel prophesied about, the foundation of which would be laid after the sixty-ninth week in the cutting off of the Messiah, and the top-stone would be added in the full end of transgression for Israel in the seventieth (Dan. 9:27).

Calvary would be *"the end of the Sabbaths"* (plural) (Mt. 28:1). From henceforth these ordinances of meat and drink, of holy days and new moons and sabbaths, were shadows fleeing away now that the substance had come (Col. 2:17). Indeed, it was the end of death, for to this purpose Christ died and rose again that He might be Lord over both dead and living (Rom. 14:9). Peter would not see the end of Jesus or of all the hopes residing in Him. All search for peace and pardon would end in Christ. Such is the merit of the cross. Let us note some of the things that were finished that day or would be, as the result of the death of the Son of God.

SCRIPTURES WERE FINISHED

Numerous passages that foretold His death, both as an atrocity and as an atonement were finished, completely fulfilled. The seeming contradictory character of these prophetic announcements is harmonized in these two aspects of our Lord's passion. Despised and rejected of men, yet heaven's chosen offering for sin. Delivered by the determinate council and foreknowledge of God, yet taken by wicked hands, crucified and slain (Acts 2:23). Cut off in the midst of His years, yet prolonging His days. Cut off and having nothing, yet seeing of the travail of His soul and satisfied (Dan. 9:26; Isa. 53:11). All these, and many other scriptures, were ended, complete in the work of the cross.

SUFFERINGS WERE FINISHED

These sufferings had begun long before His decease at Jerusalem. It was not simply that *"He hath borne our griefs, and carried our sorrows"* (Is. 53:4), a word that was fulfilled, not in His death, as advocates of "healing in the atonement" would have us believe, but in Christ's ministry of healing in life (see Mt. 8:16-17). It was also that our Lord worked with the shadow of the cross ever before Him, and worshiped with sacrifices that were acute and constant reminders of His own. One cannot read the law of the offerings today in the early chapters of Leviticus without being melted and stirred to the depths as he thinks of their terrible fulfillment in the sufferings of Christ. We have often doubted in our hearts the ability of most men, and certainly our own ability, to expound these chapters. It is like looking into the sacred ark of God.

The Messianic Psalms, too, with all their depths of desolation and humiliation, as well as the plaintive cries of the Lamentations, were to Him—whose custom was to read the prophets—terrible and exquisite anticipations of His approaching death. The three years of misunderstanding and misrepresentation, of temptation and trial, and the compressed agonies of sin-bearing were finished. He could now lay down His head and rest. Nothing but joy lay before Him who endured the cross and despised the shame.

SACRIFICES WERE FINISHED

Sacrifice and offering Thou wouldest not, but a body hast Thou prepared me...He taketh away the first, that He may establish the second. By the which will we are sanctified through the offering of the body of Jesus Christ once for all (Heb. 10:5-10).

The recurring Day of Atonement in Israel was a covering of sin, not a cleansing from it. Sins were put aside, not put away. It was impossible that the sin of a creature could be put away by the slaying of a creature. It needed Royal blood, "drawn from Immanuel's veins." By one offering He has perfected forever those who are sanctified. It is not that the sacrifice of Christ transcends the offerings offered before; it supercedes them. They are obsolete now. This offering is supreme and solitary and sufficient. The sacrifice of the Mass is an insult to God who accepted the sacrifice of the cross, to Christ who offered it, and to the Eternal Spirit through whom the sacrifice was made. The Mass denies the finality of the work of Calvary. There can be no other atonement made for sin.

SERVICE WAS FINISHED

"I have finished the work which Thou gavest Me to do" (Jn. 17:4), said the Saviour as on earth He anticipated His great intercession above. Now was finished the Father's business He declared when a boy He *"must be about"* (Lk. 2:49). Now He could lay down His head, as indeed He did (Jn. 19:30). The Son of Man could not lay His head before this.

He was going to begin another work in heaven, to prepare a place for us, to appear in the presence of God for us. This is still unfinished, but the supreme work He came to do was complete in the sixth cry of Christ, followed immediately by His death.

SATAN WAS FINISHED

Now shall the prince of this world be cast out (Jn. 12:31).

Through death He might destroy him that had the power of death, that is, the devil (Heb. 2:14).

Satan is not yet cast out, but his power is destroyed for the believer, and his doom is certain. We are not told to dread his power but are warned of his wiles.

Resist the devil and he will flee from you (Jas. 4:7).

Satan marshalled all his hosts at the place called Calvary, but the success of the cross spelled his doom. God shall bruise him under our feet shortly (Rom. 16:20).

SALVATION WAS FINISHED

Salvation in its first aspect consists in being freed from the penalty of sins. The believer sees that penalty paid, that wrath exhausted, in the triumphant cry of our Lord. The other aspects of this comprehensive term, from the power and presence of sin, follow as the result of it. We can only be saved by His life above because we are reconciled as enemies in His death (Rom. 5:10). Christ shall appear the second time unto salvation because He appeared first to put away sin.

The Greeks boasted of their power to say much in little, to put an ocean of meaning in a drop of language. Here is the greatest example of all time, a single word uttered by our Lord Jesus Christ which will take all eternity to elucidate: ***tetelestai***: *"Finished!"* The triune God finishes what He begins. Thus the heavens and the earth were finished. Propitiation was finished at Calvary, and He who begins a good work in us will finish it in the day of Jesus Christ (Phil. 1:6).

Sin was finished: *"Sin, when it is finished, bringeth forth death"* (Jas. 1:15), and the death of the Son of God will see the end of sin, as Daniel prophesied. Sin shall not have dominion over us, for He came to put it away. Being free from sin as a master, and becoming servants to God, we have our fruit unto holiness, and the end everlasting life (Rom. 6:22). Our Lord's triumphant cry for all heaven and earth and hell to hear, secures for God and for us a new heaven and a new earth wherein dwells righteousness.

All this, and infinitely more than we can possibly comprehend was finished that glorious day. May it be ours to rest in His superb achievement and to count not our lives dear unto us that we might finish our course with joy (Acts 20:24).

THE SEVENTH MESSAGE

Father, into Thy hands I commend My Spirit (Lk. 23:46).

The last word from the cross is the fitting climax to the whole. It is the grand consummation of these divine communications, the results of which are placed in the capable hands of the Father. Not only the Spirit of our Lord is committed to Him, but He is able to keep all those who have been put to sleep in Jesus (1 Thess. 4:14). The Spirit of the Forerunner here for us enters within the veil, where He Himself would soon come, and assures us of the entire preservation of body, soul, and spirit at the coming of our Lord Jesus Christ.

A communion restored— *"Father."* The old relationship at the beginning of these utterances is hereby declared again. The first cry was to the Father, the middle cry in the desolation and darkness was to God who cannot look on sin; the last cry sees the *"clear shining"* after the thunderstorm. The Victim has become the Victor; the reproach will roll away and renown take its place; the thing of shame will forever be a thing of splendor. The glad cry of *"Father"* is heard again.

Every creature bears a relation to God as Creator. But He is the Father only of those who are regenerate: *"Our Father which art in heaven..."* (Mt. 6:9). The confidence of the request is predicated on the confidence of the relationship. If that is not established, it is but taking the name of the Lord in vain. When God sends forth the Spirit of the Son into our hearts, then we cry, *"Abba, Father"* (Gal. 4:6).

A confidence restated—*"Into Thy hands..."* (Lk. 23:46). The Son of Man was betrayed into the hands of men and they killed Him (Mt. 17:22-23); He was betrayed into the hands of sinners (Mk. 14:41); wicked hands crucified Him and slew Him (Acts 2:23). Yet what are the hands of men compared to this awe-inspiring declaration?

It is a fearful thing to fall into the hands of the living God (Heb. 10:31).

But it is a blessed thing to fall into the hands of a loving Father. May we not say reverently and with bowed hearts that in the mystery of the cross, in the darkness of it, our Sin-Bearer was in the hands of the living God. In the merit of the cross we see Him in the hands of the loving Father. The difference between heaven and hell must be the difference between an unrepentant sinner falling into the hands of a sin-hating God and an obedient son falling into the hands of his Father in heaven.

Oh, the strength and tenderness of these hands! All the saints are there (Deut. 33:3). They can never perish because they are in the Father's hand (Jn. 10:29). *"Let us fall now into the hand of the Lord,"* said David, *"for His mercies are great"* (2 Sam. 24:14); and how much greater to those who live in the day of Christ.

A commission resigned. *"...I commend My Spirit"* (Lk. 23:46). This cry was a quotation from Psalm 31:5. Our Lord added the word, *"Father,"* and left out *"Thou hast redeemed me."* Redemption was in Christ Jesus. Having uttered the words, He *"yielded up the ghost"* (Mt. 27:50). Literally, Matthew says, He dismissed His spirit. It was a command as well as a committal. His decease (*exodus*) was now accomplished at Jerusalem (Lk. 9:31). Moses and Elias did not speak to the Lord about the death that would overtake Him in the "Holy City," but of the accomplishment of His exodus: His going into death and emerging triumphant from it. God would raise Him from the dead. His task was finished. He could resign His commission on earth, to assume a new one above.

Because of this we may resign our spirits also in hope of our final exodus.

> *In peace let me resign my breath*
> *And Thy salvation see;*
> *My sins deserved eternal death,*
> *But Jesus died for me!*

SEVEN

The Attraction of the Cross on Earth

And I, if I be lifted up from the earth,
will draw all men unto Me.

JOHN 12:32

Here is a superb declaration of the divine positivism, optimism, and magnetism of the Lord Jesus Christ. In the Sermon on the Mount He promulgated a higher law than that of Sinai. The words, *"Ye have heard that it was said by them of old time...but I say unto you,"* show Him speaking *"with authority and not as the scribes"* (Mt. 7:21-22, 29). What would have been supreme egotism in another was but the supreme authority and authenticity of Christ's mission.

He whom God hath sent speaketh the words of God (Jn. 3:34).

It was this devotion to His true Messiahship that left our Lord unmoved at the shouting crowd waving the branches of palm trees and crying,

Hosanna: Blessed is the King of Israel that cometh in the name of the Lord (Jn. 12:13).

On the other hand, the request of the Greeks to see Him (Jn. 12:20-21) roused in Christ the very echoings of Gethsemane. A superficial observer might have seen impressive portents of Messiah's glorious kingdom. Divine power had been evidenced in the raising of the dead; the crowd had loudly acclaimed Him King of Israel, and the Gentiles had come to worship at Jerusalem and to seek the Lord. Although it was the time of the Feast of the Passover, a time for solemn reflection and chastened spirits, the people were in the joyful mood of the Feast of Tabernacles. Zechariah, the prophet who had foretold the triumphant entry into Jerusalem (Zech. 9:9) had also pointed forward to a day still to come when the nations would come seeking the Lord, and laying hold of a Jew, as these Greeks laid hold of Philip, to effect that holy purpose (Zech. 8:23). Surely this was a fulfillment of these scriptures.

But our Lord was not impressed by this ovation. Perhaps many of these enthusiasts would soon join in another cry,

> *Away with Him, away with Him, crucify Him...we will not have this Man to reign over us* (Jn. 19:15; Lk. 19:14).

This cry for the kingdom was too premature, too superficial. In contrast, however, as we have said, the desire of the Greeks moved Christ to the depths. He had a baptism to be baptized with before these *"other sheep"* could be included in the blessing of His ministry, and again He was straitened until it was accomplished. He had been sent only to the lost sheep of the house of Israel, but the hour was come that the Son of Man should be glorified in laying the basis of His larger mission to all the world. Christ's path of glory would indeed lead to the cross and the grave, but His path to the grave would lead up to the glory.

The horror of that path to the cross, in order to draw all men to Himself, now lay heavily upon the Son of God. The language which describes it has striking parallel in Gethsemane—the troubling of the soul, the prayer to the Father, the holy resignation to the hour and the cup. The agony would increase as the cross drew near, but the elements of it were all here. The judgment of the world would be a settled thing after His passion; the Prince of this world would be cast out, but the Corn of Wheat would die to bring forth a harvest in such souls who came with the request, *"We would see Jesus"* (Jn. 12:21).

The world today, because of the culminating atrocity of Calvary, is in the position of a prisoner whose judgment has been pronounced and who is awaiting execution. Satan, on the other hand, no longer has access to heaven to accuse the brethren. The atonement of Calvary has silenced and cast out the accuser. *"Who shall lay anything to the charge of God's elect? It is Christ that died, yea rather, that is risen again...who also maketh intercession for us"* (Rom. 8:33-34). *"We have an advocate with the Father, Jesus Christ the Righteous"* (1 Jn. 2:1). Thus the atrocity of the cross accomplishes the first; the atonement of the cross accomplishes the second. It accomplishes, too, the breaking down of the middle wall of partition between Jew and Gentile. The rent veil of the Saviour's flesh burst the barriers and ended monotheistic monopolies in Israel. The Gentiles who were *"without God in the world"* (Eph. 2:12) were made near by the blood of Christ.

Thus there emerges from the context the magnetism of the cross. The One who was lifted up will draw all to Himself. The *"lifting up"* may mean more than the necessity of our Lord's death as in John 3:14; it may mean His exaltation also—*"lifted out of the earth."* He is the Sun of Psalm 19 coming out of His chamber as a Bridegroom, and as a strong Man to run the race set before Him. As the Psalmist says, nothing shall be hid from the beneficent rays of His uprising. All shall be drawn to Him. The sun smiles upon the muddy pools and changes them to clouds of fleecy loveliness. So the Sun of Righteousness arises and draws men to Himself, transforming those who respond to His love.

1. He will draw the Church to Himself. We have more than a hint of this in the raising of Lazarus (Jn. 11). It is here we have a suggestion of that later revelation given to Paul in regard to the dead and living at the coming of Christ (1 Thess. 4:13-18). The dead will rise, the living will be changed; all will be caught up in the air to meet the Lord. To Martha our Lord said,

> *I am the Resurrection, and the life: he that believeth in Me, though he were dead, yet shall he live: and whosoever liveth and believeth in Me shall never die* (Jn. 11:25-26).

Lazarus was "sleeping" and Christ came to awaken him. He came out of the tomb with the grave-clothes because he would need them again, but Christ left the clothes behind in resurrection, and so shall we. Lazarus was wakened by the commanding shout of Christ, and the sleeping church awaits the descent from heaven with a "shout of command" of the same Lord, with the voice of the archangel and with the trump of God. *"We shall not all sleep, but we shall all be changed"* (1 Cor. 15:51).

2. He will draw Israel to Himself. The raising of Lazarus may also suggest this.

> *Therefore prophesy and say unto them, Thus saith the Lord God; Behold, O My people, I will open your graves, and cause you to come up out of your graves, and bring you into the land of Israel...and shall put My Spirit in you, and ye shall live, and I shall place you in your own land...* (Ezek. 37:12-14).

After the feast of John 12:1-11, we have the triumphant entry into Jerusalem of the King of Israel. Note that the title of our Lord in chapter 11 is the Son of God, in keeping with His connection with the Church. The Church is built upon this glorious confession. But here, it is the King of Israel. The crowd cries too soon, but their act looks forward to His coming in honor to the city which once cast Him out and slew Him (see Ps. 118:22-26, from which the cry of the people is taken). The Stone which the builders rejected will then be the Head of the corner. This will be the Lord's doing, marvelous in the eyes of Israel. This will be the day that the Lord will make and His people will be glad and rejoice in it.

Israel will be gathered. It is to us a shallow exegesis that sees no glorious future for them. God has not cast away His people whom He foreknew (Rom. 11:2). In this chapter in Romans, Paul first speaks of the possibility of Israel's restoration (vv. 1-25), then of the prediction of it (vv. 25-32), then exults in praise of it, in the unsearchable wisdom, ways, and wealth of God.

3. He will draw the nations to Himself (Jn. 12:20-23). These Greeks came up to worship at the feast and then came seeking the Lord. *"We would see Jesus."* And Jesus said, *"The hour is come, that the Son of Man should be glorified."* This last title links Christ with the earth. It is noticeably absent in the epistles to the Church, but is prominent in the earthly ministry of Christ, both at the first and second advents (Mt. 24 and 25). The name *"Jesus"* could as yet bring no claim to the Lord, as coming from the lips of these Gentiles, nor any immediate response from Him other than the announcement of His impending hour of suffering to bring them to God. But the title *"Son of Man"* looks forward to that day when men of the Gentile nations shall desire to see and know Him. Then shall the prophecy of Simeon at His birth be fulfilled: *"a light to lighten the Gentiles, and the glory of Thy people Israel"* (Lk. 2:32). Revelation 7 shows a great multitude of all nations, with palms in their hands, drawn to Him.

4. He will draw all to Himself. In Mark 1:13 we read that our Lord during the temptation in the wilderness was with the wild beasts. But they lost their ferocity before "God's Millennial Man." The beasts shall share the blessing of the removal of the curse from the earth. The growls of the beasts today are their groans. The whole creation groans and travails in pain, waiting! (Isa. 11:1-9; Rom. 8:19-22). But Psalm 72 shows all gathered to Christ. This exodus portion of the psalm ends with the glories of Messiah's redemption and reign. His enemies shall be drawn for judgment to the Great White Throne after the thousand years have ended. All judgment is committed to the Son. The psalm is fragrant with millennial blessing: the earth bringing forth abundantly, the poor and needy cared for, the inhabitants of the city flourishing like the fields around them, kings from afar bringing the homage of their hearts and the bounty of their hands. All nations will be blessed in Him, the whole earth being full of His glory.

What a day for the lone Corn of Wheat that fell into the ground and died. Truly *"much fruit"* has resulted. And cannot we raise our personal testimony and say, *"He sent from above, He took me, He drew me out of many waters"* (Ps. 18:16). Verily, He drew us *"with cords of a man, with bands of love"* (Hos. 11:4) .

> I've found a Friend, O such a Friend,
> He loved me e'er I knew Him;
> He drew me with the cords of love
> And thus He bound me to Him. —*James G. Small*

In our hearts we believe that we would not have come had He not wooed us (Jn. 6:44). And we wait, with great anticipation, *"our gathering together unto Him"* (2 Thess. 2:1). We have felt the magnetic pull of the Son of Man; we shall feel it again when we are caught up to meet the Lord in the air.

EIGHT

The Acclamation of the Cross in Heaven

*And they sung a new song, saying, Thou art worthy to take
the book, and to open the seals thereof: for Thou wast
slain, and hast redeemed us to God by Thy blood out of
every kindred, and tongue, and people, and nation*
REVELATION 5:9

In this chapter it is not in the magnificence of the place
into which the redeemed are brought that declares the magnitude of the cross. Here, as elsewhere, space or time is not
taken up to describe the splendor of the appointments of
heaven, the stately beauty of the thrones, the dazzling glory
of the golden crowns. Even the city foursquare in chapter
21 is primarily a magnificent symbolic description of *"the
bride, the Lamb's wife"* (Rev. 21:9). It is common enough
in Scripture, however, for the inhabitants of a place and the
city itself to be described as one, as demonstrated in
Revelation 17:18: *"And the woman which thou sawest is
that great city which reigneth over the kings of the earth."*

The magnitude of the cross is proclaimed, first of all, in the worthiness and ability of the Lamb of God who was slain to open the Book of the counsels of God regarding earth. The voice of a strong angel searching in the respective spheres of heaven, earth, and under the earth, had failed to produce one worthy to do so.

It is manifested secondly, in the song of the elders and living creatures concerning the scope of the Lamb's redemption: *"out of every kindred and tongue and people and nation"* (Rev. 5:9).

It is indicated thirdly, in the vast company of the heavenly worshippers, myriads on myriads of the angelic host and glorified saints who cry, *"Thou art worthy...for Thou wast slain."*

It is told out finally, in the outermost circle of every creature in heaven, earth, and under the earth, and in the sea, acclaiming our gracious Lord as worthy of blessing and honor and glory and power. The magnitude of the cross is the result of the magnetism of the cross. He who was in the midst of three antagonistic circles at Calvary, as noted in Psalm 22, is in the midst of three adoring circles in Revelation 5.

In the Psalm of the Cross, He is seen compassed about by bulls of Bashan (v. 12)—ceremonially clean but apostate Israel (Amos 4:1); by the dogs—ravenous Gentiles as well as Jews; and enclosed by the satanic assembly of the wicked One. But in the vision of the Seer of Patmos, this *"same Jesus"* is in the midst of the angels, of the living creatures, and of the enthroned elders. The sacrificial Lamb who was personified by Isaiah in chapter 53, and who was identified by the banks of Jordan (Jn. 1:29), is glorified in Revelation 5. The Lord give us unshod feet, anointed eyes, and consecrated lips as we draw near to these heavenly scenes and join in the song.

"The things which are" of chapters 2 and 3, give place to *"the things which must be hereafter"* (4:1). Things present give place to things to come. This marks the third and last division of the Book of Revelation (1:19). Churches are no more seen after chapter 3. The very word disappears from the book, with the exception of the dedication of the completed volume to the churches (22:16).

At the beginning of chapter 4, John in spirit is caught up to heaven, figure of the rapture of the Church (1 Thess. 4:13-18). God is seen on the throne, dwelling in light unapproachable by created beings, yet not unmindful of His rainbow covenant with men. Its emerald character tells of its undying nature. God never forgets: *"His mercy endureth for ever."* Yet the throne is one of judicial glory, as the lightnings and voices, thunderings and fire indicate, which were present at Sinai.

The elders, however, are at perfect rest, seated on thrones, and bearing the insignia of kings and priests to God (Rev. 1:6, 5:10). The number twenty-four suggests the same that are in the gates and in the foundations of the city in chapter 21, Israel and the Church, or the redeemed from both the Old Testament and the New.

They need no cleansing, for the sea is of glass. There is no need for these priests to wash (1 Ki. 7:23). The living creatures are definitely identified with the seraphim (Ezek. 10:20; Ezek. 1; Isa. 6). There seems to us a strange reluctance to identify these living ones and endow them with the personality which these chapters in Revelation demand. Their faces show their link with all creation, and under Christ (whose fourfold presentation in the four Gospels seems to answer to those) they are custodians of the purposes of God for the earth. Michael, the archangel, on the other hand, seems to be the angelic champion of Israel (Dan. 12:1; Jude 9). Revelation 4 closes with God worshiped as Creator for whose pleasure all things were made.

Chapter 5 introduces us to the sealed book. The last chapter of Daniel makes us familiar with the figure, and that whole book deals with empires on earth and the fortunes of Israel while in their midst. The prophecies were not to take place at once; the book is sealed and shut. In Revelation 5 it is about to be opened.

We link also this passage with the closing of the book in Luke 4:16-21. There our Lord not only closed the roll of the prophecy of Isaiah which had been placed in His hands, but closed the book of the counsels of God as to judgments in the earth. He closed the prophecy after proclaiming the year of grace, and before the announcement of the day of vengeance. In the mercy of God, the year has been extended until today, but in Revelation 5 the longsuffering of the Lord is over and the day of vengeance comes.

He who closed the book on that bygone day in Nazareth now is about to open it before the assembled hosts of heaven. He who, before that day at Nazareth closed, was led to the brow of the hill to be cast down headlong, is now the judge before whose face kings and great men, as well as bondmen and free men, flee and hide themselves in the rocks and caves of the mountains. Only He who now shuts can open (Rev. 3:7). The time is ripe for the presentation of this Worthy One, whose fitness lies in His cross.

1. As we have said, the magnitude of the cross is seen in Christ's superlative fitness to open the book and dispense judgments in the earth. A strong angel with a loud voice searches heaven, earth, and under the earth, for one worthy to do so. Intelligent creation, unfallen as well as fallen, supernal, terrestrial, and infernal alike, fail to produce or qualify for the task. In the synagogue long ago, men wondered if He was worthy when He declared, *"This day is this*

scripture fulfilled in your ears." "Is not this Joseph's Son?"
(Lk. 4:21-22) they said. With the exception of some mighty
works in Capernaum, all His life of public miracles lay still
before Him. The qualifications of Luke 4:18 had not all
been manifested yet. Was He worthy?

He was. Our hearts hasten to attest it; our lips to declare
it. But only when He went to the cross could the gospel be
preached to the poor of all nations—to the broken-hearted
among all men. In Revelation 5, the cross is behind Him,
but the memory of it, the proof of it remains—a Lamb as it
had been slain. The impotence of all created beings in all
spheres to answer the strong angel proclaims that none of
them can redeem his brother nor give to God a ransom for
him. This universal inability proclaims the magnitude of
the work of Christ.

2. It is further shown in the song that bursts from the lips
of the four seraphim and the twenty-four elders. The
seraphim can join because the song is not about the favored
objects of redemption, but about the Redeemer Himself.
Here is the only One in all the universe who could redeem
and who therefore can judge. It is the world-wide character
of the redemption that is the theme of the song.

> *Thou art worthy to take the book, and to open the seals thereof: for
> thou wast slain, and hast redeemed us to God by thy blood out of
> every kindred, and tongue, and people, and nation; And hast made
> us unto our God kings and priests: and we shall reign on the earth.*
> (Rev. 5:9-10).

This appears to be the better-attested reading of the passage; the personal pronouns are thus put in the third person
and not in the first. The singers have not their own blessed
portion in mind, but the extent of the purchase which their
adorable Lord made at the cross. Even the living creatures

can join in this, which they could not if the personal results of that redemption were in view.

The Worthy One was slain. He has not conquered as the Lion; He conquered by dying. All people and nations and languages trembled and feared before Nebuchadnezzar, because whom he would he slew, and whom he would he kept alive (Dan. 5:19). But this King, of the Root of David, was slain, and out of His voluntary wounding has come blessing for all the world.

The Worthy One redeemed. All people trembled before the head of gold in Daniel, but here they fall adoring at His pierced feet and sing His praises. It is not that all the nations are saved, but out of them all the redeemed come. There is no tribe, nor nation, nor tongue, shut out from that redemption, blessed be His glorious Name.

The Worthy One has made them like Himself. They are kings and priests to God. They are not like the saved Gibeonites, mere hewers of wood and drawers of water for the favored host of the unfallen in heaven. No, they share His honor and His nature. They are like Him and with Him shall reign over the earth. They shall see the long dominion of Satan at an end, and are led from triumph to triumph in Christ. The magnitude of the cross is seen in the extent of the purchase which He made.

3. It is further indicated in the heaven-wide cry of all the angelic beings in praise to the One who was slain. They do not speak *to* the Lamb; they speak *of* Him. There is not the intimacy of the elders in speaking directly to the One in the midst, but this *"innumerable company of angels"* (Heb. 12:22) with a loud voice declare His worthiness to receive a sevenfold glory.

Some would deny that angels sing because they *"say"* in apparent contrast to those who both sing and say, but we would rather not deny this to those who in creation's glad morning sang together and shouted for joy (Job 38:7). They have more reason now, though they do not personally share in the results of redemption, nor give utterance to the result of it. They marvel and adore at the stupendous fact of their Creator's death.

4. This magnitude of the cross is noted finally in the praise of the outermost circle of all the conscious universe. According to the measure of their distant and feebler powers they render to God and to Christ a fourfold ascription of praise. They do not speak of the Lamb who was slain, but acknowledge their subjection to Him who sits upon the throne, and to the Lamb.

It would appear that this scene in heaven does not merely describe the glorification of the Lamb prior to the Tribulation when the judgments out of the book are poured forth, but embraces the final subugation of all to Christ, when to Him every knee shall bow, of things in heaven, and in earth, and under the earth, and every tongue confess that Jesus Christ is Lord, to the glory of God the Father (Phil. 2:10-11). It is common in the last book of the Bible as it is in the first, to lead on to the climax of the things just introduced, the details of which follow in succeeding chapters.

And shall we not in anticipation, even now, join the company of those who, when this last circle joins the praise, fall down and worship Him that lives for ever and ever? Amen.

NINE

The Memorials of the Cross for the Church

Baptized into His death.
ROMANS 6:3

This is My body...this is My blood.
MARK 14:22-24; 1 CORINTHIANS 11:24-25

The true believer always has before him the memorials of the cross. The use he makes of the ordinances of baptism and the communion of the bread and the cup, not the things themselves, constitutes the remembrance. To him these emblems are meaningless unless accompanied—in fact, preceded—by faith in the Christ of whom they speak.

In Scripture, baptism is associated with the preaching of the gospel, and accompanied by marks of faith in those who were the subjects of it. This is best seen by reading through the Acts of the Apostles and noting carefully those who were baptized and when.

Scripture, too, will show the wide gulf that separates the

simple memorial instituted by the Lord Himself in the Upper Room and carried out by the Church, and the elaborate ritual, the vestments, ceremonies, and officialism that go on today in many places.

The memorials of the cross for the observance of the Church are these two: baptism and the Lord's Supper. We must not add to these the keeping of days and months, and times and seasons, being foreign to the spirit of the present age (Gal. 4:10-11). We may well take advantage of these traditional occasions to proclaim the truths of Christ's cross, and to rejoice in the triumphs of His resurrection, but they are not sacred days in the biblical calendar of the Christian Church.

1. "BAPTIZED INTO HIS DEATH" (Rom. 6:3-4)

Know ye not, that so many of us as were baptized into Jesus Christ were baptized into [unto] His death? Therefore we are buried with Him by baptism into death...

Romans 6 logically follows the truth of the two Headships of 5:12-21, and identifies the kind of baptism here. In the one man, Adam, all died, for all have sinned. By one man's disobedience the many in him are constituted sinners (not merely sinful), and by the one Man's obedience the many in Him are constituted righteous. All in Christ live, for His death is their death. They have died to sin in Christ who died unto sin once. Thus where death has reigned as a king for so long, grace has come to reign. Where sin abounded grace did much more abound.

This naturally (for the human heart either resists grace or misunderstands it) raises the question in Romans 6:1. *"Shall we continue in sin, that grace may abound?"* Does not man's greater sin call forth God's greater grace—the more sin, the more grace? Why, then, seek to escape from the power of indwelling sin? Paul meets this with an emphatic refusal and refutation, and reminds his readers of the illustration of Christian baptism. They were baptized as identified with Christ their Head. In Him they died to sin: in Him they rise to walk in newness of life. The ordinance sets this forth. The baptism of the Spirit is not in the context here. His baptism is not unto death, but into the Body of Christ. Our identification in Christ's death is the subject to which our baptism clearly points.

In the apostles' day the faith which received the message concerning Christ immediately showed itself in baptism. The words *"so many of us"* in verse 3 do not mean that some were not baptized who had believed. The words are equivalent to, *"**all we who were** baptized into Christ Jesus were baptized into His death."* Unbaptized believers are not contemplated in the New Testament. Baptism is so closely associated with faith that the latter is inherent in the record of the carrying out of the ordinance itself (Lk. 7:29-30; Acts 22:16; Gal. 3:27).

Paul has not abandoned his theme in Romans chapter 6 (where the theme is justification by faith) and substituted baptism, reminding those who happened to be baptized of the meaning of the rite. To Paul it was the very sign of faith, which all who believed had shown. In that faith they had died with Christ; they were buried with Him in baptism. It was not so much that they saw an end of their sins in the atoning blood of the Saviour, but rather that they saw an end of sin, of themselves the sinners, in that death.

The objective results of the death of Christ for the believer are stated first in this chapter. A glance at the Revised Version of this passage will show that the tenses used indicate past acts. The personal experiences of the believer are not here, but rather what is true indeed of all believers. They have died unto sin. The old man is crucified. They were planted (united) with Him in the likeness of His death.

Later on, the apostle shows the subjective side. They were to reckon themselves to be dead indeed unto sin. They were to yield themselves unto God as those alive from the dead. They were to obey from the heart the mold of doctrine into which they were delivered. In this way they would walk about in a new kind of life (Rom. 6:4) and adorn the doctrine so eloquently declared in their baptism.

Thus the ordinance becomes a memorial indeed. We do not look back to the past act of our baptism in complacency, but always have before us the challenge of living as those dead unto sin but alive unto God.

Each baptism we witness should bring before us in a fresh way our Lord's death unto sin once and His life unto God. Remembering that with many of those *"baptized unto Moses"* God was not well pleased (1 Cor. 10:1-12), we take heed lest we fall. At all times we shall have before us in baptism the burying of our old standing in Adam, and our new standing in Christ—

> ...*that as sin hath reigned unto death, even so might grace reign through righteousness unto eternal life by Jesus Christ our Lord* (Rom 5:21).

2. "This is My Body...This is My Blood."

"This do in remembrance of Me." The second memorial of the cross is variously called the Lord's Supper, the Breaking of Bread, and the Communion. The Eucharist is a name suggested by the word in the Greek language for "giving of thanks" (see 1 Cor. 11:20; Acts 2:42, 20:7; Mt. 26:26-28; Mk. 14:22-24; Lk. 22:19-20; 1 Cor. 10:16-17; 1 Cor. 14:16).

The early Church recognized no other ordinances than the two we have indicated. Our Lord's words, *"Ye also ought to wash one another's feet"* (Jn. 13:14) were not taken by the early disciples as indicating an ordinance for the Church, as its history will bear witness.

The things we use in this memorial are bread and wine. The mere use of these elements themselves do not constitute a memorial. Like the ordinance of baptism, they cannot be divorced from a living faith. Some eat and drink condemnation to themselves, not discerning the Lord's body (1 Cor. 11:29). The Supper was instituted on the night of our Lord's betrayal. It is Luke who tells us that it was His desire that His disciples continue to observe it as a remembrance of Himself. The Church accordingly did so and celebrated it on the first day of the week (Acts 20:7).

Whereas baptism was an ordinance accomplished once upon confession of faith in Christ, and can only be regarded as a memorial, the Lord's Supper was a regular observance in the primitive Church—indeed we may say authoritatively, a weekly observance. It was ordained to bring continually before the believer the basis of all his blessings—the death of Christ.

As originally given by our Lord, it was simplicity itself. Nothing was prepared especially for the occasion; nothing was created at the feast. The common things that were on the table at the Passover served to institute the present sacrament. There was no "consecration of the elements," either by our Lord or later by the apostles. In none of the passages listed at the beginning of our subject is it indicated. The *"blessing"* of the bread in Matthew and the *"giving of thanks"* for the same in Luke show the interchangeableness of the terms. The same exchange of words is seen in the accounts of the feeding of the four thousand, when our Lord gave thanks for the loaves and blessed the fishes. In the Corinthian passages, *"we"* bless the cup (ch. 10) and Jesus our Lord gave thanks for the bread (ch. 11). Nor is there proof that those who thus *"bless"* in 1 Corinthians 10:16 are the apostles or their successors, for the *"we"* of verse 16 are those of verse 17 who make up the one body and who partake of the bread. There is no case here for the sacerdotalist.

This simplicity is further marred by any suggestion of transubstantiation or any related transformation being in the Saviour's words. It is representation and not transformation. In the passage in 1 Corinthians 11, it is clear that after the *"blessing"* or giving of thanks, it is still referred to as the bread and the cup. It is not *"as often as ye eat My body and drink My blood,"* but *"as often as ye eat this bread and drink of this cup."* The simple-hearted followers of Christ had no such pagan notions of "eating the god" which later influenced Christianity when it had spread its branches and sheltered the fowls of the air. Their Lord held the bread in His hand. The hand was distinct from that which it held.

"This is My body." The use of such metaphors is common enough in Scripture. *"The seven good kine are seven years"* (Gen. 41:26). *"These bones are the whole house of Israel"* (Ezek. 37:11). Sarah and Hagar are two covenants (Gal. 4:22–24). *"The seven heads are seven mountains"* (Rev. 17:9). In these passages there is no need of a qualifying statement that the things present represent something else. The *"are"* is the equivalent of "represent."

Note, too, that in the passages in the Gospels dealing with the Supper, the *"cup"* is the covenant in Christ's blood, but we know it is intended that we should understand the cup to mean its contents, the fruit of the vine.

It need hardly be said, too, that the simplicity is still further spoiled by the intrusion of elaborate ritual or peculiar vestments, and the necessity of some priest other than one who shares it in common with all the believers.

The passage in 1 Corinthians 11 reveals the proper perspective in the celebration of this memorial of the cross.

THE LOOK UP: OUR AUTHORITY

"For I have received of the Lord that which I also delivered unto you" (1 Cor. 11:23). Like the gospel Paul preached, he neither received it of men nor was taught it, but by the revelation of Jesus Christ (Gal. 1:12). Paul did not go to Jerusalem to those who were apostles before him, who might conceivably have taught the erstwhile persecutor the doctrines they held dear. He rather went to the solitude of Arabia where alone with his Lord he might gather the far-reaching implications of his evangel. Part of this was the reiteration of Christ's desire to be remembered in the Breaking of Bread. Had the Lord's Supper been of a transitory character, as some would affirm—not to be continued as soon as the Church was established—our Lord would have made it known to *"the apostle of the Gentiles."*

On the contrary, Paul writes to the Corinthians and emphasizes the divine authority of the Communion. We might safely reason too, that the same authority for the ordinance of baptism was given to the apostle at the same time, since he in this same letter mentions having baptized certain believers. The context (1 Cor. 1) shows baptism was in his program, as it was in that of all the apostles, though not in his personal practice of the rite, lest he be charged with baptizing in his own name.

Peter seems careful also to have others do the actual baptizing, as seems clear from Acts 10:48. Neither Peter nor Paul deemed that apostolic hands were necessary to the carrying out of the rite. It is blessed to look up to the Lord alone for our authority in taking these plain symbols into our hands. It is *"of the Lord."* It is divine in origin.

THE LOOK BACK: OUR APPRECIATION.

Ye do show the Lord's death... (1 Cor. 11:26).

The brethren of Joseph never forgot his request concerning his bones, but carried them in all their journeys until they buried them in Canaan. They always bore about with them the dying of Joseph until they were home in the land of promise.

Israel never forgot the vanished glory of Jerusalem as they lovingly fingered the great stones of the ancient walls.

> *If I forget thee, O Jerusalem, let my right hand forget her cunning. If I do not remember thee, let my tongue cleave to the roof of my mouth: if I prefer not Jerusalem above my chief joy"* (Ps. 137:5-6).

A matter of bones and a matter of stones, but the saviour of Egypt and the city of the great king will still be held in affectionate remembrance. And shall they shame us who have a Person to remember, the glorious Person of the Saviour of all men, especially of those that believe? The place was everything to the Jews; the Person is everything to the Christian. One place and one alone was hallowed by the divine presence in Israel; no spot above another is thus hallowed for the Church. Wherever two or three are gathered in His Name, there He is in the midst, but He seems to come closer when He makes Himself known in the Breaking of Bread.

With our hearts gratefully contemplating Calvary and with the bread and wine in our hands, He seems to show us afresh His hands and His side. Thus we, too, go about ever bearing the dying of the Lord Jesus, and when our hearts are warmed in this way, we feel like whispering for His ear alone, "If I forget Thee, O Christ, let my right hand forget her cunning. If I do not remember Thee at this supreme moment, let my tongue cleave to the roof of my mouth: if I prefer not Thee above my chief joy."

THE LOOK AHEAD: OUR ANTICIPATION

Ye do show the Lord's death, till He come (1 Cor. 11:26).

Our wandering has an end; the long road has a terminus: "till He come." Like Joseph's brethren we shall one day lay away the memorials for the last time. *"Until Shiloh come,"* said Jacob, and *"unto Him shall the gathering of the people be"* (Gen. 49:10). That was the prophecy!

And every one that was in distress, and every one that was in debt, and every one that was discontented, gathered themselves unto him (1 Sam. 22:2).

That was the picture! *"Our gathering together unto Him"* (2 Thess. 2:1). That is the prospect! *"I will overturn, overturn, overturn it...until He come whose right it is; and I will give it Him"* (Ezek. 21:27). The feast must go on until He come.

THE LOOK IN: OUR ATTITUDE

Let a man examine himself, and so let him eat of that bread and drink of that cup. For he that eateth and drinketh unworthily, eateth and drinketh damnation to himself, not discerning the Lord's body (1 Cor. 11:28-29).

The attitude of our hearts is important. We need to bring to the feast the preparation of the whole life of the week that has gone by. We cannot be on the Lord's Day what we are not on the other days of the week.

Worship is neither workshop nor wash-up. We cannot work ourselves into a speedy attitude of worship, nor be in the Spirit with a tardy confession of our sin just before the divine celebration.

We need to be aware of the fowls of the air which come down when we are laying bare the holy things of the sacrifice of our Redeemer (Gen. 15:11). Abram drove the unclean birds away. So we need to beware of the vulture of uncleanness which would intrude in our holiest moments.

The eagle eye of criticism for those who come in late, for what people are wearing, or for what they will say, spoils many a hallowed hour.

The raven of black despair and doubt and anxiety often flies in, and we take careful thought for the things of the morrow when we should be in the peace and worship of the present. The sacrifices of the Old Testament brought sins to remembrance, but the sacrifice of Christ brings Him to remembrance. We are not in the presence of the king to remember our faults (Gen. 41:9).

The peacock of pride and complacency robs us of the preciousness of the occasion. Beware the attitude that thinks, "We are in the place where the Lord has placed His Name; others are not. They are of Paul, or Apollos, or of Cephas; we are of Christ. They are the denominations; we are unsectarian. They only have Communion once a quarter; we have it every week."

The sparrow of familiarity, however, may come in here. Perhaps it is the fear of this diminutive fowl of the air that other churches have the feast less frequently. Are we better than they if we are more scriptural but less spiritual? If it is mere custom and not Christ, if our baskets are empty when we come (Deut. 26:1-10), if we examine not our manner of living and our motives before we come, we shall fail to discern the Lord's body, and eat and drink unworthily.

The "look in" is not that we should stay away, but that we should come. We shall never be worthy in ourselves, but in Christ. We can only sacrifice that which has cost us something. Shall I give to the Lord that which cost me nothing? This sanctified introspection will be the best preparation for the retrospective and anticipative views we take as we sit before the Lord, and hear Him say, *"This is My body...this is My blood"* (1 Cor. 11:24–25).

TEN

The Brand Marks of the Cross in the Believer

I bear in my body the marks of the Lord Jesus.
GALATIANS 6:17

The marks of the cross are for us also. The Lord Jesus shall bear in His body forever the marks of His cross, His crucifixion.

In Exodus 21 there is the law of the Hebrew slave. He was to serve six years and go out free in the seventh. If he was married when he came, his wife was to go out with him. If, however, his master had given him a wife, she was to remain, with any children that had come as the result of this union. If the slave for love to his wife and children, and above all to his master, desired to remain, his ear was bored in token of his perpetual servitude. *"He shall serve him for ever"* (Ex. 21:6). *"For ever"* could only indicate his lifetime on earth, but as typical of Christ who took upon Himself the form of a bondslave (Phil. 2:5-8) the words indicate that the marks of His servitude are forever.

The Lord God hath opened (bored) *mine ear, and I was not rebellious, neither turned away back* (Isa. 50:5).

Sacrifice and offering thou didst not desire; mine ears hast thou opened (bored) (Ps. 40:6).

For love to God, to His bride, and to all the children God gave Him, our blessed Lord took the place of a bondman. The marks of this will send us adoringly to His pierced feet throughout eternity. His will be the only scarred body then. *"Behold,"* said He in resurrection, *"My hands and My feet"* (Lk. 24:39). John beheld a Lamb as it had been slain (Rev. 5:6). The marks remain.

Similarly, if we have taken our cross and borne it, we will have the marks of our crucifixion upon us at the present time. If at Calvary we've "adoring stood and gazed at that wondrous cross" we have heard Him say, *"If any man will come after Me, let him deny himself, and take up his cross daily and follow Me"* (Lk. 9:23). When you take up your cross you are on your way to death, to crucifixion. Paul looked upon himself as a crucified man. Galatians is the Epistle of Crucifixion.

1. It is here we read that when Paul came to these simple country people he set Jesus Christ before them crucified (Gal. 3:1). The words here convey the idea that Paul graphically portrayed the crucifixion before them. As the local magistrate publicly placarded the death of a prisoner, Paul vividly set forth the fact and blessed results of the death of Christ.

What had been to the Jews a stumbling block and to the Greeks foolishness, had been readily received by these demonstrative souls. The seed fell, not in deceived hearts by the wayside, nor in distracted hearts among thorns, but in the demonstrative hearts of the stony ground. The

Galatians were fervent but fickle. They took the messenger of the cross to their hearts and would have plucked out their own eyes and given them to him, but their growth was stunted and their running hindered by legalism. His epistle, written in haste and in heat, was to bring them back to the simplicity of their first faith and fervency.

2. It is here we read of Paul's personal crucifixion (Gal. 2:20). *"I am crucified with Christ."* There was a time when the "I," the ego, was very marked in Saul of Tarsus. We get a glimpse of this in Philippians 3:4-6. He had built his barns and was proud of them. But the day came when he pulled them down to build greater ones for eternity. The "I" bent over until it became a "C." His former life lay in shattered fragments at his feet. Henceforth it was no longer I but Christ. *"I am crucified with Christ: nevertheless I live."* Paul's desires were at an end; he would live only unto Him who died for him and rose again.

3. It is here we read that *"they that are Christ's have crucified the flesh with the affections and lusts"* (Gal. 5:24). The context here has to do with the works of the flesh and the fruit of the Spirit. The one we restlessly pursue; the other is borne by us independent of our striving. It is produced by the walk in the Spirit.

If we live in the Spirit we are to walk by the Spirit. It was a great discovery for Paul when he learned that Christ died, not only for what he, Paul, had done, but for what he was—not only for his sins, but for sin. In Romans 3:25 and 4:7 it is sins; in chapter 6:1, 2, 6 it is sin.

Shall we continue in sin...? God forbid! How shall we, that are dead to sin, live any longer therein? Knowing this that our old man is crucified with Him... (Rom. 6:1-2, 6).

He that has died is acquitted from sin. Being made free from sin as a master, we have become the servants of righteousness.

These great objective facts of the death of Christ must first be learned before the apostle will show us the subjective side of our reckoning, our obeying, our dethroning. God desires that the cross be the end of us. The works of the flesh give way to the fruit of the Spirit; to the walk in the Spirit. They that are Christ's can only show it by living in *"the new kind of life"* of Romans 6:4.

The word *"walk"* in Galatians 5:16 suggests it is not an enthusiastic bound that gets you to a certain place, a spiritual attainment, but a spiritual adjustment of the life day by day.

4. Finally, it is here that we read that the world was crucified to Paul and he to the world (Gal. 6:14).

> *But God forbid that I should glory, save in the cross of our Lord Jesus Christ, by whom the world is crucified unto me, and I unto the world.*

By virtue of that cross the world had nothing for Paul and Paul had nothing for the world. He began this epistle by telling us that Christ gave Himself that He might deliver us from this present evil age. It was not enough that God would *"pass over"* Israel in Egypt; they must pass over into the wilderness from Egypt. This was the salvation of which God spoke and of which they sang on the other side of the Red Sea. *"...Till Thy people pass over, O Lord, till the people pass over which Thou hast purchased"* (Ex. 15:16). Paul had grasped this purpose; the world spread its charms in vain for him.

The Galatians were victims of a subtle transplantation of Judaism to their young life in Christ. They were foolish in giving up grace for law, freedom for bondage. Were they the spiritual children of Ishmael, not Isaac? Was their mother Hagar, not Sarah? Were they the progeny of Sinai, not Sion? Their principle and position were false; their practice was foolish as a result. Those who had taught them and enslaved them were perverters of the gospel, deserters from Christ. The poor Galatians were but mutilating the flesh in a meaningless circumcision.

As Paul is about to lay down his pen after his indignant remonstrance, he seems weary.

Henceforth let no man trouble me, for I bear branded on my body the marks of Jesus" (Gal. 6:17, ASV).

It was as if he said: I have marks in my flesh of my perpetual servitude to the Lord Jesus. What have these Judaizing teachers to show for their fealty to Him?

Of the Jews, five times received I forty stripes save one,. Thrice was I beaten with rods. Once was I stoned: thrice I suffered shipwreck; a night and a day I have been in the deep, in journeyings often, in perils...in weariness and painfulness, in watchings often, in hunger and thirst, in fastings often, in cold and nakedness... (2 Cor. 11:24–27).

Paul's brands were real; circumcision a useless mutilation for these Gentile believers. A slave's brands were the marks of ownership. Paul's were far more. They were the scars of experience, of veterancy, of devotion, of commission. What could the false teachers show? What could the Galatians? What can we?

God will not look us over for medals but for marks; not for badges but for brands; not even for our theological degrees, but for the bored ear, the wearied body, the consecrated hands and feet. The unbelieving world still cries, *"Except I shall see the print of the nails...I will not believe."*

The Epistle to the Galatians indicates these marks: fruit-bearing (5:22-23); burden-bearing (6:1-10); brand-bearing (6:14-17). Thus the self-life, the life towards others, and the life towards God will find truest and fullest measure through the cross of our Lord Jesus Christ.

FRUIT BEARING: THE PERSONAL LIFE (GAL. 5:19-23)

The manifestations of the flesh are plainly indicated in the passage as they are in us. The list shows grosser sins at the beginning and the end, and in between are those things which we consider not so serious and are therefore often unjudged. But God has placed them in the middle, so that they shall not escape us. Our hearts recoil from the first and the last, but what about quarreling, jealousy, anger, rivalry (strife), dissension, party-spirit, envy? These are also the deceitful manifestations of an unsatisfied heart—the works of the flesh.

But the fruit (singular) of the Spirit is wrought in us. Abiding in the Vine, walking in the Spirit, fruit is brought forth in a nine-fold cluster independent of our striving. There seems parallel as well as antithesis in the two lists, the first and the third distinct from the second. This fruit will be seen in love, joy, peace, faithfulness, gentleness, and self-control in ourselves, and patience, kindness, and generosity toward others.

While the first three can only be fully appreciated by the eye of God, the last three may be apparent to the eyes of men. Patience, kindness and generosity are the good works which are seen of men and glorify our Father in heaven.

BURDEN-BEARING: THE LIFE TOWARDS OTHERS (GAL. 6:1-10)

"Bear ye one another's burdens" (Gal. 6:2). The burden of verse 2 is not the same as the burden of verse 5. In the latter, the word used indicates the personal load (responsi-

bility) of the child of God, both here and at the Judgment Seat of Christ. Some have likened it to the soldier's pack which he personally must carry. But verse 2 indicates something weighty, a burdensome thing which our brother or sister is striving to shoulder and which we are called to bear. Like Issacher we must, in the best sense of the words, crouch between two burdens, our own and our brother's, and bow our shoulders to bear (Gen. 49:14-15).

We shall find, contrary to carnal thinking, that there is rest in so doing. *"And he saw that rest was good and the land that it was pleasant"* (Gen. 49:15). *"Ye shall find rest unto your souls. For My yoke is easy, and My burden is light"* (Mt. 11:29–30).

Verse 1. My brother may suddenly be caught in a trespass and bear a burden of remorse, *"swallowed up with overmuch sorrow"* (2 Cor. 2:7). I am to restore him, to mend the dislocation, as the word means, the continuous present tense being used to show the gentleness and perseverance required. If I consider myself above such a continuous and humbling ministry, I should note verses 3-4.

Verse 6. My brother who ministers the Word may have a burden. The Levites of old bore the *"burden"* of the tabernacle (Num. 4:46-47), and in times of departure from God they were often forgotten as to their need.

Since the people began to bring the offerings into the house of the Lord, we have had enough to eat, and have left plenty (2 Chron. 31:10).

The minister of the Lord has the promises of God, but God may use us to bear what may at the moment be a heavy burden of need. Our duty is to minister to them in material things as they have ministered to us spiritually.

Verses 7-8. These verses we often hurl at the head of the sinner; let us note they are written to sons and in connection with our liberality. *"He which soweth sparingly shall reap sparingly. He which soweth bountifully shall reap also bountifully"* (2 Cor. 9:6). He who sows not at all to the Spirit but to the flesh can only reap that which the flesh inevitably leads to—corruption,

Verse 10. Even unbelievers are not to be overlooked in this divine bearing of burdens. We are to do good unto all. Our clusters of fruit must reach over the wall, as Joseph's, the fruitful bough (Gen. 49:22). He was the saviour of the world as well as of his household. Good works, in the first and last mention of them in the New Testament, are for the world and not for our own (Mt. 5:16; 1 Pet. 2:12).

Meantime, we are not to be weary in well-doing, either at the lack of appreciation, or at the poverty of results. We may often feel we have labored in vain and spent our strength for nought, yet surely our judgment is with the Lord and our work with God (Isa. 49:4). In due season we shall reap. In the meantime, it is our responsibility to bow our shoulders to bear.

BRAND-BEARING: THE LIFE TOWARDS GOD. (GAL. 6:17)

"Let nobody trouble me after this, for I carry on my body the scars that mark me as Jesus' slave" (Williams Trans.). These brands were not the marks of circumcision which the Galatians had foolishly made themselves subject to. These were the deeper marks of Paul's servitude to Christ. It is not our talk about being crucified with Christ and to the world; it is the inner mark of the reality of that slavery. Have we any wounds to show, marks of experience, devotion, sacrifice?

God give us "plainly" to say, *"I love my Master, my wife, and my children; I will not go out free"* (Ex. 21:5) and to go to the door for the bored ear. How good is the rest of His burden; how pleasant is the land where we thus dwell.

ELEVEN

The Ministry of the Cross Today

...to preach the gospel: not with wisdom of words, lest the cross of Christ should be made of none effect.

For the preaching of the cross is to them that perish foolishness; but to us which are saved, it is the power of God...And I, brethren, when I came to you, came not with excellency of speech or of wisdom, declaring unto you the testimony of God. For I determined not to know any thing among you, save Jesus Christ, and Him crucified.

1 CORINTHIANS 1:17-18; 2:1-2

The Church's message to the world is the ministry of the cross. With Paul it was a ministry of reconciliation, a ministry to testify the gospel of the grace of God (2 Cor. 5:18; Acts 20:24). It must emulate the great apostle, not only in the matter of its evangel, but in the manner and motive of it. The context of the above quotations furnishes us with these.

The first Corinthian epistle gives us the divine order in the Church, but prefaces it with the divine origin of the

Church's message. The factions of the church in Corinth were because they had failed to grasp the factor of the cross. They were exalting the messengers over the message.

Because of this, the apostle, before he speaks of their exaltation of human leaders, emphasizes the exaltation of the divine Lord. Observe the full titles, *"the Lord Jesus Christ," "Jesus Christ our Lord."* He is mentioned in every verse (1 Cor. 1:1-10). He was not only their Saviour; He was their Sovereign.

He is seen in these verses as their sanctifying, unifying, and satisfying portion. If they were designated *"church of God"* it was because they were sanctified in Christ Jesus, called saints. If they were associated with others, it was because commonly they called upon the name of Jesus Christ their Lord. If they came behind in no gift, it was because they were enriched by Him in all utterance and in all knowledge. Their expectation was the revelation of the Lord Jesus Christ. It was all Christ. Who then was Paul or Apollos, but ministers (deacons) through whom they believed (1 Cor. 3:5)? There was no place for factions in the Fact of Christ. It is then that the apostle speaks of the cross, what it was and was not, according as it is viewed from the estimation of God or of the world, from the estimation of the perishing or the experience of the saved.

THE MINISTRY OF THE CROSS: ITS MATTER

The gospel had nothing in common with the wisdom and philosophies of men. It was opposed to everything that men took pride in. Cicero, though he lived before Christ, declared that the cross spoke of what was so shameful and horrible it ought never to be mentioned in polite society. Later orators and philosophers echoed his words and applied them to the cross of Christ. It put no premium on human wisdom, but discounted it entirely. Philosophy then, as now for the most part, was a desperate human attempt to account for a universe apart from a Creator. If it acknowledged a Creator at all, He must not be allowed to act as an omnipotent Creator should. He was shackled with the laws He Himself ordained. His gospel must flatter the human ego and laud human effort in salvation. Christianity must be an academic question for the philosopher.

But the questions are raised here: where is the thinker, the writer, the learned disputer? God passes them all by and chooses, not many wise, not many mighty, not many noble. The five things He chooses in 1 Corinthians 1:27-28 are in keeping with the lesson we learn from the use of number five in Scripture—weakness in connection with man; grace in connection with God.

The gospel was not espoused at the beginning by clever thinkers, by wealthy patrons, by clever propagandists. The preachers' message was of the shameful death of a felon of a subject nation. It had nothing naturally for the Roman who loved power, for the Jew who loved ritualism in religion, for the Greek who loved wisdom.

It brooked no rivals, which was contrary to the Roman idea of annexing all the gods of the heathen and adding them to their own impressive list. It called upon the Jew to forsake an elaborate ritual for a simple service. It called upon the Greek who lauded virtue and practiced vice, who exalted the mind and so often debased the body, to discount his wisdom and confess his guilt. Salvation was not by thinking but by believing. The Roman despised it, the Jews stumbled themselves upon it, the Greeks accounted the preaching of the cross foolishness. The matter of the apostolic message ran counter to them all.

We need to remember this today. We are not personally greatly impressed with the valiant attempts to square science with Scripture. It seems to degenerate into an attempt to square Scripture with science. Scientists, many truly Christian, in their fields of geology, botany, or biology, seem to recognize their classifications' forms and orders in the simple but comprehensive language of Genesis 1, and speak triumphantly of the striking way that Scripture conforms to science. To us, to whom it is not the wisdom of the world, but the wisdom of the Word, it is so much the worse for science so-called if it does not ally itself with revelation. Science has had to defend itself against the charge of continually shifting ground. It is constantly molting, and while this is a sign of growth, it is not maturity. The Bible, on the other hand, is a full-grown revelation, and the cross the supreme event of the fullness of the times (Gal. 4:4).

THE MINISTRY OF THE CROSS: ITS MANNER

The brilliant apostle to the Gentiles, so far from coming to Corinth radiating self-confidence, came in weakness, and in fear, and in much trembling (1 Cor. 2:3). After his experience in Athens he was desperately anxious that his personality should not intrude between souls and his message. He determined to know nothing save Jesus Christ and Him crucified. He would preach, not with enticing words of man's wisdom, but in demonstration of the Spirit and of power. He would not, if he could, pander to popular taste, that the faith of the Corinthians should not stand in the wisdom of men.

Paul spoke words of wisdom, but not with wisdom of words. Those weak and foolish and base and despised things of chapter 1 that God had chosen would become the *"perfect,"* the mature of chapter 2:6, under those words of wisdom. As those who were distressed and in debt and discontented—a motley crowd gathered themselves unto David and he became a captain over them, making them swift, and strong, and skillful (1 Sam. 22:1-2; 1 Chron. 12:8), so those gathered to Christ, regarded by the world as weak and foolish and base, are made mature by the Word and Spirit of the Lord.

The lowliness of the beloved apostle and the loftiness of the Corinthians are in contrast in chapter 4. They were full; the messenger of the cross knew hunger and thirst. They were rich; the men who brought them the gospel were naked. They were reigning as kings; the apostles had no certain dwelling-place. They were wise; the preachers were fools for Christ's sake. They were strong and honorable; but the messengers weak and despised. Being defamed, they entreated; being reviled, they blessed; being persecuted, they suffered it. In all things they approved themselves as ministers of the new covenant, and walked in the footsteps of the Lord.

And the cross must be ministered by men of like manner. Self-aggrandizement and self-gratification have no place in the proclamation of the cross and no example in its early ministers. Only in the measure that we are nothing is the cross everything. Ezekiel must not be content to stand in the river with the water up to the ankles. He must go forward, led by the man with the line in his hand, until he is lost sight of completely. God's river of grace must not only engage us, it must engulf us (Ezek. 47).

THE MINISTRY OF THE CROSS: ITS MOTIVE

Both the manner and motives of Paul are brought out more fully in his second epistle to the Corinthians, the key-word of which is *ministry*. He was keenly aware of the personality of Satan and of the opposition of many of the Corinthians as his instruments. This opposition showed itself in questioning the motives of the apostle, as well as his credentials. This grieved his sensitive soul and forced him to such a vindication as made him regard himself as a fool.

I am become a fool in glorying; ye have compelled me: for I ought to have been commended of you: for in nothing am I behind the very chiefest apostles, though I be nothing (2 Cor. 12:11).

"In the sight of God" is a phrase repeated in the book which brings out Paul's manner and motive.

For we are not as many, who corrupt the word of God: but as of sincerity, but as of God, in the sight of God speak we in Christ (2:17).

His preaching was not like those who having food to sell in baskets, put the best on top, which is what the word translated "corrupt" means. Sincerely, in the sight of God, the apostle has spoken.

...by manifestation of the truth commending ourselves to every man's conscience in the sight of God (2 Cor. 4:2).

Paul's practice ought to have commended itself to every man's conscience as it did his own. He always provided for things honest in the sight of the Lord and of men (2 Cor. 8:21). *"...I wrote unto you...that our care for you in the sight of God might appear unto you"* (2 Cor. 7:12).

Paul's pastoral care is seen in the matter of the erring brother of whom he had written. The primary purpose of his letter was neither the cause of the injured nor the injurer, but to demonstrate his loving interest in them.

Neither Titus nor Paul had made gain of them at any time as Paul could testify before God in Christ (12:18-19).

Thus in his preaching life, his public life, his private life, his pastoral life, Paul was above reproach. Being in the sight of God it was not *"after the flesh"* (1:17; 5:16; 10:2-3). Paul neither walked nor warred after the flesh. His movements were carefully weighed in the balance of the sanctuary. His motives were always before him, the love of Christ constraining, holding him down to that life of self-lessness, as he went from place to place. He always had the sentence of death in himself (1:9).

Thus the ministry of the cross demands the holiest and humblest of manner, the loftiest of motives, the deepest consecration of methods. We need to dwell much in the second epistle to the Corinthians that we might challenge our own authority and motives. How do we measure up to great passages like chapters 1:12, 17; 4:2, 10; 5:9; 6:3-10; 8:21; 10:13-16; 11:2, 7-9, 23-29; 12:10, 15; 13:9? And when we have done so, let us *"examine ourselves whether we be in the faith"* of such an one—whether we are the seal of someone's apostleship in the Lord (2 Cor. 13:5; 1 Cor. 9:2).

TWELVE

The Preachers of the Cross

Ye are witnesses, and God also, how holily and justly and
unblameably we behaved ourselves
among you that believe.
1 THESSALONIANS 2:10

The character of the messengers must always be the
highest credential of their message. Our messages fail in
power to others because they fail in practice in ourselves.
The gospel of the Crucified needs a crucified man to proclaim it.

In the first Thessalonian epistle we see that the converts
in chapter 1 were what they were because the preachers
were the men that they were in chapter 2. As in the physical, so in the spiritual, there is a likeness, an affinity
between fathers and those who are begotten of them. The
gospel came not to these Thracians in word only, but also
in power, in the manifested power of the Holy Spirit. They
knew what manner of men the apostles became among
them (1 Thess. 1:5).

The conduct of Paul and Silas and Timothy, the men who
brought the message to the Thessalonians, is brought out in

detail in chapter 2. There it is seen that they came as evangelists (1 Thess. 2:2-6), and remained as pastors (1 Thess. 2:7-8), and teachers (1 Thess. 2:11-12).

The boldness of the evangelists is reflected in the sounding out of the word by the converts. The conduct of the fathers is reproduced in the children, so that they *"were examples to all that believe in Macedonia and Achaia"* (1:7). They knew something of the fellowship of the sufferings that always accompanies faithful witness for God.

The Thessalonians were at once earnest in their witness, exemplary in their walk, eager in their waiting. Their attraction was real: they turned to God from idols. Their allegiance was real: they served the living and true God. Their anticipation was no less genuine: they *"wait[ed] for His Son from heaven"* (1 Thess. 1:10).

Here we read that they were *"dear"* to the servants of God, a word translated *"beloved"* elsewhere, and in turn the apostles did not need to write to them to love one another. They had been taught of God to do so (4:9).

It is a solemn thought that our converts take shape from us. They seem, however unwittingly, to *"become followers of us,"* and if we are not followers of the Lord, as the apostle states in chapter 1:6, we shall mislead them.

A harsh, critical, sectarian spirit is often seen in the spiritual children of one who himself is of this unholy disposition. Thank God that the prayerfulness of a Hannah may be reproduced in a Samuel, the profound regard of a Mary for the holy Scriptures (as seen in her song) is repeated in the desire of her Son that *"the Scripture might be fulfilled."* The unfeigned faith of a Lois, of a Eunice, may be seen in a Timothy.

The qualifications for all messengers of the cross come out in seven statements in chapter 2. These statements sum up the manner, matter, and motive of these early pioneers.

While there is a categorical denial of the sevenfold charge made upon them by their enemies—that of deception, uncleanness, fraud, men-pleasing for base gain, flattery, covetousness, glory-seeking—there is also in the seven things the positive declaration which was true of those primitive propagators of Christianity. Note, *"we were bold," "we were allowed"* (approved), *"we were gentle," "we were willing," "we would not be chargeable," "we behaved ourselves," "we exhorted, comforted, charged every one of you."* When we measure up to these qualifications, we have the credentials of the messengers of the cross.

WE WERE APPROVED (1 THESS. 2:4)

We take this one first as preparatory to the whole. A glance at the Revised Version will show the word *"allowed"* is *"approved."* It occurs also at the end of the verse and is translated *"trieth"* our hearts.

The messengers were not novices. Paul, separated from birth and called by grace to preach (Gal. 1:15), was proved some ten years after conversion before being called to the work in Antioch (Acts 11:25-26). His ministry in Antioch, during which time he visited Jerusalem again and came back to labor with Barnabas and Mark, may have occupied a further three or four years, so that there was perhaps a period of fourteen years from the time his ministry to the Gentiles was announced until his missionary call to perform it.

Silas was not a novice. He is mentioned as a chief man among the brethren and was chosen to accompany Paul and Barnabas with the good news of the happy concurrence of the church at Jerusalem with Gentile inclusion and liberty in Christ (Acts 15) .

Nor was Timothy one lately come to the faith and upon whom hands were laid suddenly. From a child he had known the holy Scriptures and by them was made wise unto salvation. He was well reported of, not only in his own city, but in a neighboring one, and was chosen by Paul to the band of fellow workers (Acts 16:1-3; 2 Tim. 3:14-15).

Each of these men had been proved and approved locally before being sent out to a wider sphere of service. They were *"entrusted"* with the gospel. Surely men of like caliber should have this stewardship entrusted to them today.

The emphasis, however, must be on the state of the heart and not of the head (v. 4). It is the heart that God approves. Nothing but a true state of heart could make Paul write after ten years of association with Timothy that his young yoke-fellow naturally cared for the Philippians when all others were seeking their own. Timothy was still serving as a son with a father in the gospel (Phil. 2:20-22). Modern messengers of the cross are approved men.

WE WERE BOLD (1 THESS. 2:2)

The shameful treatment at Philippi did not deter these early messengers. They did not feel that they ought to lie low for some time after the beating and stocks and imprisonment. Their insult as Roman citizens did not breed either a desire for vengeance or a desire to avoid a similar occurrence in the next city they visited. They left Philippi and went down the highway to Thessalonica.

The word translated here *"shamefully entreated"* means insult or bodily injury, and may well cover both. *"They have beaten us"*—that was the injury; *"openly uncondemned, being Romans"*—that was the insult. The magistrates themselves had to come and beseech the prisoners to come out and to depart from the city. Unhurried, the evangelists came out, visited the house of Lydia, and departed for the next scene of their fruitful labors. Opposition would be as great in Thessalonica, but these courageous men went in with the emancipating message.

We need bold men and women today, but they must be *"bold in our God."* We allow the fear of man to intimidate us more than we realize, but the Lord can give us that courage to go back to the place where of late, they sought to stone us (Jn. 11:7-8).

> *Now when they saw the boldness of Peter and John...they marvelled; and they took knowledge of them, that they had been with Jesus* (Acts 4:13).

See also Acts 14:19-20 where the apostles went back to the city—back, if need be, to the stones, to the insult and the injury.

WE WERE GENTLE (1 THESS. 2:7)

"Gentle...as a nurse cherisheth her children." Here is the tenderness of love. Moses' mother was paid to nurse her own baby. If Hatshepsut, Pharaoh's daughter, did not know she had hired the mother of the baby she had found by the flags of the river, she would soon have discovered it had she watched the face of the nurse. The love-light in her eyes would soon have betrayed the fact that she was cherishing her own child.

Paul and his brethren were among the Thessalonians as nurses, "feeding and keeping warm," as the word means, those who were their own babes in Christ.

Missionaries of the cross must be gentle men, and not simply what passes for gentlemen. Their boldness must never degenerate into harshness, or their courage into coarseness. They must not think that masculinity means masterfulness. *"The servant of the Lord must not strive, but be gentle unto all"* (2 Tim. 2:24).

Later in this chapter, we shall see the discipline of love, as a father deals with his children; here is the tenderness of love, as a nursing mother cherishes her own children.

WE WERE WILLING (1 THESS. 2:8)

The word *"willing"* here means more than a conscientious impulse to bring them the good news of the gospel. It means a pleasurable and continuous determination to share with them not only the gospel, but their very lives. How genuine the affection of the apostles; how generously Paul wrote of his companions.

David's mighty men were willing men, particularly those who broke through the host of the Philistines and brought him a drink of water from the well of Bethlehem. He had longed for the water he had often refreshed himself with in his boyhood. The men did not receive a command; it was a thing pleasing in the sight of their master and it touched David's heart (see 1 Jn. 3:22). They had done it willingly because he was dear to them.

Messengers of the cross must be willing persons. Only their *"affectionate desire"* will make them willing. As the tense of the word shows here, it will not be a sudden impulse in a burst of enthusiasm, but an impelling thing that will carry them on day after day.

Like Jacob, their heart will lift up their feet. *"Did not our heart burn within us...and they rose up the same hour, and returned to Jerusalem"* (Lk. 24:32-33). Men with approved hearts will always be willing men; therefore they should keep their hearts with all diligence.

WE WOULD NOT BE CHARGEABLE (1 Thess. 2:9)

The glory Paul mentions in verse 6 very probably includes material gifts (Gen. 31:1; Ps. 49:16). The apostles of Christ might have been chargeable to the church at Thessalonica, but they forewent their lawful claims to silence detractors and to be an example to the believers, some of whom Paul had to rebuke in each epistle for failing to labor with their hands to provide for their own needs (2 Thess. 3:7-12).

Nehemiah and Paul walked the same path and breathed the same spirit.

> *Moreover from the time that I was appointed to be their governor in the land of Judah, from the twentieth year even unto the two and thirtieth year of Artaxerxes the king, that is, twelve years, I and my brethren have not eaten the bread of the governor. But the former governors that had been before me were chargeable unto the people, and had taken of them bread and wine, beside forty shekels of silver; yea, even their servants bare rule over the people: but so did not I, because of the fear of God* (Neh. 5:14-15).

This sacrificial spirit of the cross must be upon the messengers of it. Surely its preaching must never enrich the preachers. He who enriches himself under guise of preaching about Him who was rich but for their sakes became poor, is a disgrace to the cause he professes to espouse. The highest type of service we can render the Lord must be that which would lead us to labor with our own hands that we might not be chargeable to any. The brother who thus labors must not be regarded as inferior to him who, because of more abundant labors, is dependent on gifts or stipend for his maintenance.

Nor should those out "in faith" regard it as a breach of trust on the part of God or men, if the exigencies of their path cause them so to labor with their own hands to carry on the work. With such examples as these before them, they must rejoice to be in the sacred succession.

Our trust must be in God, not in men. The Lord of the Harvest might want His *"laborers"* to do a little labor with their hands, as the apostles did, to supply not only their own need, but the need of those with them (Acts 20:34).

WE BEHAVED OURSELVES (1 THESS. 2:10)

Actually the word *"behave"* does not occur in the passage. The apostle simply says that in a holy, righteous, unblameable manner they were among them. It is the same as chapter 1 verse 5, where it is translated *"came"* and *"were."* Also John 1:14 where the *"Word was made flesh."*

This conduct both God and the Thessalonians were called to witness. In verse 5, they could judge the apostles' words, but God alone could judge their motives. Here in verse 10 both God and men are called to witness that the behavior of the apostles *"adorned the doctrine"* of God our Saviour in all things.

These men sought, whatever the charges made by evil men, to walk in holiness towards God and blamelessly before men. Crusaders of the cross must behave themselves. Like creation in Psalm 19, their witness can be unceasing though unuttered. Their character will speak loudly and its sound reach to the end of the earth.

What a tragedy when after having preached to others, the missionary himself is disapproved and has to be recalled.

Only let your manner of life be worthy of the gospel of Christ, so that whether I come and see you or else be absent, I may hear of you that you stand fast in one spirit, with one mind striving side by side for the faith of the gospel (Phil. 1:27; RV. See also 2 Cor. 1:12).

We Exhorted and Comforted and Charged
(1 Thess. 2:11)

Here is the mature and perhaps sterner character of the missionaries' ministry of love among the Thessalonians. They had exhorted them, *"calling them alongside"* as the word means, to pursue the same path as the messengers. They had comforted or encouraged them, and they had *"charged"* them, a word which means that they had witnessed to them by their lives as well as by their word.

This stirring up, binding up, and building up was all the discipline of love by men who could say that their absence from their converts was a bereavement from them (1 Thess. 2:17). The word *"taken"* is the word from which we have *"orphan"* and it reveals the throbbing hearts of those first messengers of the cross.

By men of this caliber the work was established two thousand years ago and made such converts among the Thracians. By such men churches are formed today and built up in their most holy faith. The glorious ministry of the cross needs consecrated men to proclaim it.

God make us these men. God make us earthly vessels fit to contain this priceless treasure of the ministry of the cross. The superlative glories of the cross call for superlative representation on the part of its ambassadors, and superlative efforts to make these glories known. We must not fail.

Scripture Index